The Genius of
GEORGE WASHINGTON

EXITUS ACTA PROBAT

George Washington

EDMUND S. MORGAN

W · W · NORTON & COMPANY

NEW YORK · LONDON

The Third

GEORGE ROGERS CLARK LECTURE

17 November 1977

The Clark Lectures of the Society of the Cincinnati are presented on subjects relating to the American Revolution. It is not contemplated that the lectures will constitute fresh contributions to the scholarship of the American Revolution, but rather that they will interest and inform a lay audience, and perhaps stimulate some to undertake and enjoy independent reading on the Revolution.

Though these endowed lectures honor General Clark, they are not necessarily expected to touch upon or refer to that officer or the military operations of his command.

Copyright © 1980 by Edmund S. Morgan
Published simultaneously in Canada by George J. McLeod Limited, Toronto.
Printed in the United States of America
All Rights Reserved

ACKNOWLEDGEMENTS

"The Houdon bust of Washington," photograph through the
Courtesy of the Mount Vernon Ladies' Association of the Union.

Library of Congress Cataloging in Publication Data
Morgan, Edmund Sears.
The genius of George Washington.

Includes bibliographical references and index.
1. Washington, George, Pres. U.S., 1732–1799—
Addresses, essays, lectures.   2. Presidents—United
States—Biography—Addresses, essays, lectures.
I. Title.
E312.63.M839   1981   973.4'1'0924   [B]   80–26763
ISBN 0–393–01440–1
ISBN 0–393–00060–5 pbk.

W. W. Norton & Company, Inc. 500 Fifth Avenue, New York N.Y. 10110
W. W. Norton & Company Ltd. 25 New Street Square, London EC4A   3NT

1 2 3 4 5 6 7 8 9 0

CONTENTS

WHEN A CROWD OF AMERICAN FARMERS OPENED fire on the regular troops of the British army some two hundred years ago, the action must have seemed foolhardy to any impartial observer. Such an observer might have been a little surprised at the events that immediately followed, when the farmers put the regulars to rout, chased them from Concord to Boston, and laid siege to that town. But however impressive this performance, it did not alter the fact that the British army was probably the most powerful in the world, having succeeded scarcely a dozen years before in defeating the armies of France, England's only serious rival. For a handful of colonists, unorganized, without any regular source of arms or ammunition, with no army and no navy, to take on the world's greatest power in open war must still have looked like a foolhardy enterprise.

Somehow or other it proved not to be. Yet it remains something of a puzzle that the farmers were able to bring it off. With the benefit of hindsight we can offer a number of explanations. For one thing, the generals whom the British sent to put down the rebels proved to be somewhat less than brilliant in using the immense force at their disposal. For another thing, the colonists got a great deal of assistance from England's old enemy, France. But perhaps most important, the Revolution seems to have elicited from those who participated in it a response that no other event or situation in American history has been able to do.

It was not that extraordinarily large numbers of people were ready to sacrifice their lives or their fortunes for the common good. That has often happened in times of crisis. And the Revolution did not in fact induce this kind of sacrifice very widely. It was always difficult to fill up enlistments in the Continental Army. What was extraordinary about the Revolution was the talent it generated, the number of men of genius who stepped out of farmyards and plantations, out of countinghouses and courtrooms, to play a leading role in winning the war and then in building a national government.

People noticed this from the beginning. Already in the summer of 1775 members of the Continental Congress were observing that "Times like these call up Genius, which slept before, and stimulate it in action to a degree, that eclipses what might before have been fixed as a Standard."[1] Fourteen years later, looking back on the crowded events that had followed, David Ramsay of South Carolina reflected that the Revolution had "not only required, but created talents." Men, he said, "spoke, wrote, and acted, with an energy far surpassing all expectations, which could be reasonably founded on their previous acquirements."[2] And indeed if one were to make a list of the great men of American history, by whatever standards one chooses to measure greatness, an astonishingly large proportion would be found whose careers began or culminated in the Revolution. It would be hard to find in all the rest of American history more than two or three men to rank with Washington, Franklin, Jefferson, Hamilton, Madison, or John Adams.

To say this does not bring us any closer to an explanation of why the Revolution created such an array of talent. If we knew what the conditions were for generating talent of this kind, we ought all to be busy trying to reproduce them, for we certainly need it now. Unfortunately I do not know how the Revolution generated talent. But I do want to take a close look at the talents of the man who has always stood foremost in the galaxy of Revolutionary heroes and who more than any other single man was responsible for bringing success to this seemingly foolhardy enterprise, the American Revolution. I cannot say how George Washington acquired the abilities and the character to achieve what he did, but I would like to try to say where I think his special genius lay, what his genius was and how it operated.

This is not an easy task, for George Washington is and was a hard man to know. Part of the difficulty in approaching him comes from the heroic image in which we have cast him and which already enveloped him in his own lifetime. But it is not simply the plaster image that stands between him and us. We have other national heroes who also became legendary figures in their own lifetimes, a Benjamin Franklin, an Andrew Jackson, an Abraham Lincoln; and yet with them we find no great difficulty in pushing past the image to find the man. In their letters and other writings, in the countless anecdotes they inspired, we can meet them on familiar terms and feel comfortable in their company.

But not George Washington. The familiar anecdotes about Washington tell us to keep our distance. The most arresting one is told about a gathering at the time of the Constitutional Convention in 1787. One evening during the sessions of the Convention a group of Washington's old friends from wartime days were remarking on the extraordinarily reserved and remote manner he maintained, even among his most intimate acquaintances. And the men I am speaking of considered themselves to belong in that category. One of them, Gouverneur Morris, who was always full of boldness and wit, had the nerve to disagree with the rest about Washington's aloofness. He could be as familiar with Washington, he said, as with any of his other friends. Alexander Hamilton called his bluff by offering to provide a dinner with the best of wine for a dozen of them if Morris would, at the next reception Washington gave, simply walk up to him, gently slap him on the shoulder, and say, "My dear General, how happy I am to see you look so well." On the appointed evening a substantial number were already present when Morris arrived, walked up to Washington, bowed, shook hands, and then placed his left hand on Washington's shoulder and said, "My dear General, I am very happy to see you look so well." The response was immediate and icy. Washington reached up and removed the hand, stepped back, and fixed his eyes in silence on Morris, until Morris retreated abashed into the crowd. The company looked on in dismay, and no one ever tried it again.[3]

It seems today a rather extravagant reaction on the part of our national hero, a bit of overkill. It makes us almost as embarrassed for Washington as for poor Morris. Yet it may serve us as an appropriate starting place for our inquiry, because Washington's dignity and reserve, the aloofness that separated him from his contemporaries and still separates him from us, were, I believe, an integral part of the genius that enabled him to defeat the armies of Great Britain and to establish the United States as an independent world power.

Washington's genius lay in his understanding of power, both military power and political power, an understanding unmatched by that of any of his contemporaries. At a time when the United States needed nothing quite so much as military power but had very little, this hitherto obscure Virginia planter knew how to make the best possible use of what there was. And after securing independence, when the United States was trying to establish itself in a war-torn world, he knew how to deal with foreign countries to the maximum advantage of his own. He was not a bookish man. He contributed nothing to the formal political thought of the American Revolution, nor did he produce any treatises on military strategy or tactics. But he did understand power in every form.

At the simplest level Washington's understanding of power showed itself in the ability to take command. Some men have the quality; others do not. Washington had it, and in exercising it he nourished the aloofness that became his most conspicuous visible trait. That aloofness was deliberate, as I think it may be in many men who have the gift of command. One thinks, for example, of Sir Francis Drake. In Washington it may have grown around a nucleus of inborn native reserve, but Washington purposely cultivated it. We should not mistake it for arrogance. Washington did crave honor and pursued it relentlessly, but he did not deceive himself with that spurious substitute for honor, which is arrogance. His aloofness had nothing to do with arrogance. It had to do with command.

He explained the matter in a letter to a fledgling colonel in the Continental Army in 1775: "Be easy and condescending in your deportment to your officers," he wrote, "but not too familiar, lest you subject yourself to a want of that respect, which is necessary to support a proper command."[4] Eighteen years later he gave his plantation manager at Mount Vernon the same advice for dealing with the overseers beneath him. "To treat them civilly," said Washington, "is no more than what all men are entitled to, but my advice to you is, to keep them at a proper distance; for they will grow upon familiarity, in proportion as you will sink in authority."[5]

Washington practiced what he preached, and as his talents for command developed there were fewer and fewer persons with whom he could allow himself to be familiar. As commander in chief and later as president, he could scarcely afford it with anyone. The remoteness that still surrounds him was a necessary adjunct of the power he was called upon to exercise.

But Washington's understanding of power went far beyond mere posture. Although he had not had a great deal of military experience before he took charge of the Continental Army in 1775, his participation in the French and Indian War from 1754 to 1758 had exposed him to the geographical conditions of warfare on the American continent and the way in which they must affect the exercise of military power. As commander of the Revolutionary army he was quick to perceive the significance of geographical factors that his opponents seem never to have grasped. At the outset of the war, when the British almost caught him in the Battle of Long Island, he learned the danger of allowing his forces to be bottled up in any location where their retreat might be cut off. Having learned that lesson, he did not make the same mistake again. Though he was not always able to prevent his subordinates from making it, his constant alertness to it enabled him to keep his precarious army in existence. In September, 1777, for example he sent a letter on the subject to Brigadier General Thomas Nelson in Virginia. In the light of future events it was a remarkable letter. Nelson had proposed to station his forces at Hampton and Yorktown, which lay at the end of the peninsula between the James and the York rivers. Here, of course, they would be in a position to observe the movement of any British troops into the area by sea. But the location, Washington perceived at once, was one where they could be trapped, and he quickly warned Nelson against it. The troops, he said, "by being upon a narrow neck of land, would be in danger of being cut off. The Enemy might very easily throw up a few Ships into York and James's river, as far as Queens Creek; and land a body of men there, who by throwing up a few Redoubts, would intercept their retreat and oblige them to surrender at discretion."[6] Four years later Lord Cornwallis made the mistake that Washington warned Nelson against, and Washington pounced. It was almost like taking candy from a child. For Cornwallis it was the world turned upside down, but for Washington it was a lesson learned long before in the geography of power.

Of course, if the British navy had been on hand in

sufficient strength, Cornwallis might have escaped by sea. But Washington did not move until he had the French navy to dominate the seas nearby. He had realized early in the war that without local naval superiority to stand off the British warships, he could not capture a British army at any point on the coast. Washington understood this better than his more experienced French helpers. The Comte de Grasse, in command of the French navy, seems to have missed the whole point of the Yorktown strategy, complaining to Washington that he would prefer to cruise off New York where he might encounter the main British fleet, rather than be an idle spectator in the Chesapeake.[7] Washington knew, however, that even with de Grasse on hand, he was not strong enough to have attacked the main British force in New York. But by picking off Cornwallis at Yorktown he could deal the British a crippling blow.

Washington's appreciation of geographical factors made him not only wary of being trapped like Cornwallis but also averse to defending any particular point, including cities. The British armies were much more powerful than his and capable of taking any place they wanted. It was therefore not worthwhile to erect elaborate stationary defenses. When General Howe was approaching Philadelphia and Congress wanted Washington to divert troops to the preparation of fortifications for the city's defense, he refused. If he could defeat Howe in the field, he said, the defenses would be unnecessary. If he could not, then the time and labor spent on them would be lost, for the fortifications would sooner or later fall to Howe's superior forces and could then be used against the Americans.[8] Washington knew that possession of the town would not affect the outcome of the war in any case. By 1778 he thought the British too had learned "that the possession of our Towns, while we have an Army in the field, will avail them little.... It is our Arms, not defenceless Towns, they

9

have to subdue."[9] Washington had certainly learned this, but the British had not.

Nor had many Americans, who were always calling upon Washington to detach troops for protection of particular areas. Washington generally refused the requests in polite explanatory letters to the governor of the state that was involved. It was imperative, he believed, to keep his small force concentrated and mobile, so that he could strike effectively when opportunity presented. "It would give me infinite pleasure," he assured the Congress, "to afford protection to every individual and to every Spot of Ground in the whole of the United States."[10] But that was not the way wars were won. Wars were won by destroying or disarming the enemy, not by trying to spare civilians from occupation. And Washington was bent on winning.

Washington, in other words, was or became a good field general. But his understanding of military power did not stop at the ability to command troops and deploy them effectively. He also understood that the power he could wield in battle depended on the willingness of the civil government to supply him with men and money. He understood the political basis of military power, and he also understood that in the new United States this was a very precarious basis. His army was the creature of a Congress that never quite dared to act like a government. Congress declared independence. It authorized the creation of the army. It even authorized the creation of a navy. But it did not attempt to levy taxes to pay for these things. Instead, it recommended to the states that they make contributions, specifying the amount for each state. Whether a state followed the recommendation depended on how its legislature felt at the time. Ultimately it depended on public opinion. And public opinion was as fickle then as now. Rumors of peace and of British surrender came with every skirmish, and each one produced a

10

debilitating effect on the willingness of taxpayers in the different states to advance money for a war that might soon be over.

Men were almost as hard to get as the money to pay and clothe and feed them. As a result Washington was never able to build an army strong enough to face the British on even terms. At the outset of the war he had hoped to enlist soldiers for the duration. Instead, Congress provided for enlistments of a year only. It took almost that long to collect and build a disciplined fighting force, even from men who already knew how to fire a gun. By the time he had them trained, their terms would be up, and off they would go, frequently taking with them the guns he had issued them. In their place would often come raw militia on even shorter terms, men who were not used to obeying commands and who did not take kindly to them, men who were ready to head for home and tend the crops the moment they were offended by some officer's efforts to bring them in line. In 1780, after the war had dragged on for five years, Washington was still trying to get Congress to place the army on a more lasting basis. He put the case to them in a recital of the evils brought on by their shortsightedness:

> To one who has been witness to the evils brought upon us by short enlistments, the system appears to have been pernicious beyond description.... It may easily be shewn that all the misfortunes we have met with in the Military line are to be attributed to this cause. Had we formed a permanent Army in the beginning, which by the continuance of the same men in Service, had been capable of discipline we never should have had to retreat with a handful of Men across the Delaware in Seventy Six; trembling for the fate of America, which nothing but the infatuation of the enemy could have saved. We should not have

11

remained all the succeeding Winter at their mercy with sometimes scarcely a sufficient body of Men to mount the ordinary Guards, liable at every moment to be dissipated, if they [the enemy] had only thought proper to march against us. We should not have been under the necessity of fighting at Brandywine with an unequal number of raw Troops, and afterwards of seeing Philadelphia fall a prey to a victorious Army. We should not have been at Valley forge with less than half the force of the enemy, destitute of every thing, in a situation neither to resist nor to retire. We should not have seen New York left [by the enemy] with a handful of men, yet an overmatch for the main army of these States....We should not have found ourselves this Spring so weak as to be insulted by five thousand men, unable to protect our baggage and Magazines, their security depending on a good countenance and a want of enterprize in the Enemy. We should not have been the greatest part of the War inferior to the enemy, indebted for our safety to their inactivity, enduring frequently the mortification of seeing inviting opportunities to ruin them, pass unimproved for want of a force which the Country was completely able to afford.[11]

Although Washington's complaints to Congress were fruitless, he never appealed over the heads of Congress to their constitutents. He refrained from doing so in part because the very effort to explain the situation to the public would also have explained it to the enemy. He did not dare to advertise the weakness of his force, when the only thing between him and defeat was the fact that the enemy did not realize how weak he was.[12] But his restraint was also based on principle. In spite of the imperious manner with which he bolstered his ability to command, Washington was a republican. He had been fully per-

suaded that the king of England and the minions sur-
rounding him were conspiring to destroy the liberties of
Americans.[13] More than that, he was persuaded that kings
in general were a bad lot. He welcomed Thomas Paine's
devastating attack not only on George III but on monarchy itself.[14] He never doubted that the United States must
be a republic. And the principles of republican liberty as
he saw them dictated that the military must be forever
subordinate to the civil power. Although he could lament
the short-sightedness exhibited by Congress and the state
legislatures, he never even suggested that he and his army
should be anything but their servants.

Washington realized that he could have commanded
an immense popular following in defiance of the do-
nothing congress and that he could have counted on the
backing of his officers and troops in such an adventure.
But he accepted the premises of republican government as
an Oliver Cromwell never did. Although it meant submit-
ting to a body that became increasingly incompetent, ir-
responsible, and corrupt, he never sought power on any
other terms than those on which he had initially accepted
it, as servant of the people. And when his men grew
exasperated with the failure of the government to feed,
arm, or pay them, he stood between them and Congress
and thwarted every threat against the civil power. Enlisted
men mounted mutinies, and he faced them down with his
steely authority. Some of his officers conspired to seize
power, and he nipped the movement in the bud. When
one of them hinted to him in a letter that the country
would be better off with Washington running it instead of
Congress, he rebuked him in a message assuring him that
he "could not have found a person to whom your schemes
are more disagreeable."[15]

Washington was fighting not simply for independence
but for an independent republic. He was fighting a

people's war, and he knew that he would lose what he was fighting for if he tried to take more power than the people would freely give. One of the difficulties of republican government, as he explained later to uncomprehending foreigners, was that the people have always to feel an evil before they can see it. "This," he admitted, "is productive of errors and temporary evils, but generally these evils are of a nature to work their own cure."[16] In the end, he believed, the people would do the right thing. Washington's patience in waiting for the people to do the right thing is the more remarkable, because he knew that the ineffectiveness of Congress not only prolonged the war needlessly but also exposed the country to needless perils. Because Congress lacked the nerve to vote him the needed men and money, he had to rely on assistance from the French in order to bring the war to a successful conclusion. And reliance on the French could have meant the loss of the very independence Americans were fighting for.

It was perfectly good politics, of course, to seek help against England from England's traditional enemy, and Washington welcomed assistance in the form of arms and ammunition. But he had also to rely on French troops and the French navy. There lay the danger. Once French forces were engaged on the American continent, Washington feared that they would wish to invade and occupy Canada. Ostensibly the United States would be the sole beneficiary of such a move, for the French agreed to forego any territorial claims on the continent in their treaty of alliance with the United States. But Washington had no illusions about the binding power of treaties.

Unfortunately Congress did have illusions. At the beginning of the war Americans had hoped that Canada would join them in rebellion against England, and Washington himself thought it highly desirable to eliminate this bastion of British power. He had sent an expedition to effect the liberation of the province, but the inhabitants had not responded in the manner hoped for, and the expedition was a disaster. With the arrival of French troops, Congressmen developed an enthusiasm for trying again with French forces. The population of Canada was mainly French, and it was plausible to suppose that they would welcome their countrymen more warmly than they had the Americans. But Washington was alarmed. He would not have been in a position to refuse if the French had decided to employ their troops in this way, but he did not want Congress encouraging them to do so. He wrote out all the tactical reasons he could think of against the expedition and sent them in an official communication to Congress.[17] Then he wrote out a private, confidential letter to Henry Laurens, the president of Congress, explaining his real objection. The letter remains one of the more striking examples of the quick perception of political realities that lay behind Washington's understanding of power.

The expedition, he explained to Laurens, would mean "the introduction of a large body of French troops into Canada, and putting them in possession of the capital of that Province, attached to them by all the ties of blood, habits, manners, religion and former connexions of government. I fear this would be too great a temptation to be resisted by any power actuated by the common maxims of national policy." He went on to outline all the economic and political benefits that France would gain by holding on to the province in violation of the treaty. It would not be difficult to find a plausible pretext. The United States had borrowed funds from France on a large scale; and the United States government, if one could dignify Congress by that name, had no power to tax its citizens in order to repay the debt. The United States could scarcely object if France retained Canada as security for the payment. "Resentment, reproaches, and submission" would be the only recourse left to the United States. And Washington went on to read a gentle lecture to the gullible members of Congress: "Men are very apt," he said, "to run into extremes; hatred to England may carry some into an excess of Confidence in France; especially when motives of gratitude are thrown into the scale. Men of this description would be unwilling to suppose France capable of acting so ungenerous a part. I am heartily disposed to entertain the most favourable sentiments of our new ally and to cherish them in others to a reasonable degree; but it is a maxim founded on the universal experience of mankind, that no nation is to be trusted farther than it is bound by its interest; and no prudent statesman or politician will venture to depart from it."[18]

Congress never learned the maxim, as it demonstrated by instructing its envoys in the final peace negotiations to follow the dictates of the French court. The independence of the republic owed much in the end to the wisdom of men who understood the interests of the people better than their elected representatives did.

Washington himself never departed from the maxim that he had urged on Henry Laurens, and it served him well when he became President of the United States. But before looking at his achievement in that position, we may notice one final area of his understanding of military power. As he understood the political basis of military power, so also he understood, far better than Congress did, its economic basis. He looked upon the small troop quotas and short-term enlistments provided by Congress as a squandering of manpower and financial resources. By such timidity, he pointed out, "we have protracted the War, expended Millions and tens of Millions of pounds which might have been saved."[19] What he was saying, in modern terms, was that Congress had paid no attention to the cost-effectiveness of its measures. Had it drawn on the country's resources in effective amounts, it could have won the war in two years at half the expense required to keep it going for eight.

Washington's objection to the use of militia also had an economic basis. It was not merely their ineffectiveness in the field that bothered him but the fact that military service carried them away from their farms and thereby reduced the country's food production. They were ever eager to leave the field and get back to the fields. Washington would rather have had them stay there in the first place and grow food for him if Congress had only allowed him to recruit an army that would stay with him.[20]

As the half-hearted war gradually depleted the country's resources, Washington accepted the reality and called upon Congress to borrow money abroad in order to get the thing over with.[21] He did not worry about the nation's capacity to pay back what it borrowed. The long-range economic potential of the country was enormous. Its population was growing exponentially. But as the war dragged on, he saw that the outcome might hinge on which side could keep on paying the bills.[22] He feared it might not be the United States, dependent as it had become, for the short term at least, on the treasury of France. In a shrewd economic comparison of America's enemy and America's ally he concluded that England, with a larger commerce than France, though much smaller in population, had the larger resources. "Though the government is deeply in debt and of course poor, the nation is rich and their riches afford a fund which will not be easily exhausted. Besides, their system of public credit is such that it is capable of greater exertions than that of any other nation.... France is in a different position. The abilities of her present Financier have done wonders. By a wise administration of the revenues aided by advantageous loans he has avoided the necessity of additional taxes. But I am well informed, if the war continues another campaign he will be obliged to have recourse to the taxes usual in time of war which are very heavy, and which the people of France are not in a condition to endure for any duration."[23] It was a prescient analysis. The victory at Yorktown came in time to prevent an immediate testing of the economic strength of the two countries, but not in time to prevent the fiscal exhaustion that eight years later required the calling of the French Estates General, the starting point of the French Revolution.

With the victory at Yorktown and the peace that followed, the United States had no further need of the military wisdom of which it had made such poor use. But Washington as a civilian was no less cogent in his understanding of power than he had been as commander in chief. His response to the postwar vicissitudes of the nation matched that of the most constructive political thinkers on the scene, and his influence may have been greater than theirs because of the enormous prestige he now carried.

The ineffectiveness of Congress that had hampered Washington's prosecution of the war continued to threaten the viability of the new republic in peacetime. Having submitted to the military loss of her mainland colonies, England set about to regain them by economic warfare, or so it seemed. In the early years of peace English merchants, offering liberal credits, sent shiploads of goods to their old customers in America, and Americans rang up a huge debt. But when Americans tried to ship their own goods to their old prewar markets in the British West Indies and elsewhere, England closed the ports to them. Before the Americans could gain new outlets for their produce many found themselves bankrupt. Washington's reaction was that power should be met with power. If England barred American ships, Americans should bar

English ships until England relented.[24] But for some states to do so and others not would defeat the strategy, and Congress had no authority to regulate trade for the whole nation. Washington supported every move to give it such authority, but at the same time he despaired of putting power in the hands of men who had demonstrated again and again their timidity in using it. What was the use of giving them more powers, he asked, when "the members seem to be so much afraid of exerting those which they already have, that no opportunity is slipped of surrendering them, or referring the exercise of them, to the States individually?"[25]

Washington had been convinced, long before the war ended, that the national government as it operated under the Articles of Confederation was not adequate to carry out its functions; and he feared it had in effect written its own death warrant by failing to exercise what powers it had. "Extensive powers not exercised," he once observed, "...have I believe scarcely ever failed to ruin the possessor."[26] But he hoped against hope that this would not be the case with the United States. When the inhabitants of western Massachusetts rose in arms against their own elected government in Shays' Rebellion, and neither the state nor the national government seemed ready to do anything about it, it looked as though the case was hopeless. Henry Lee urged Washington to use his influence to quiet the troubles, but Washington snapped back, "Influence is no Government....If they have *real* grievances, redress them....If they have not, employ the force of government against them at once."[27] It was mortifying to see the new American republic exhibiting the weakness that doctrinaire European political philosophers had always attributed to republics. "How melancholy is the reflection," Washington wrote to James Madison, "that in so short a space, we should have made such large strides towards fulfilling the predictions of our transatlantic foe! 'leave them to themselves, and their government will soon dissolve.' ...What stronger evidence can be given of the want of energy in our governments than these disorders? If there exists not a power to check them, what security has a man for life, liberty, or property?"[28]

But the weakness of the American republic did not diminish Washington's republican ardor. He was outraged by the very idea of rebellion against a republican government, but he was also outraged by the reaction of Americans who talked without horror of substituting a monarch for the ineffective Congress. And after the Massachusetts government finally succeeded in putting down the rebels, he objected to the fact that they had been disfranchised. To deprive them of political rights was as much an abuse of power as the failure to use power effectively against them in the first place.[29] Fortunately a number of other Americans were as disturbed as Washington about the impotence of the national government and the impending dissolution of the union. When they met together in the Constitutional Convention to seek a remedy, it was inevitable that they should choose him to preside; and when the resulting Constitution was adopted it was also inevitable that the people should choose him to preside over the new government it established. He thus gained the opportunity to demonstrate to his countrymen, as well as to the skeptics of the Old World that a republican government could show as much energy as any other.

Washington brought to the presidency of the United States a determination to establish what he called "a national character," by which he meant something like national reputation. It was essential, in his view, that the country gain a reputation that would oblige other countries to respect it. "We are a young Nation," he had written in 1783, "and have a character to establish. It behoves us therefore to set out right for first impressions will be lasting, indeed are all in all."[30] And in the years that followed the winning of independence, as the power of Congress continued to wane, his great worry had been that the failure of the states to support the union would "destroy our National character, and render us as contemptable in the eyes of Europe as we have it in our power to be respectable."[31] With an effective national government in operation at last, it became possible to establish a proper national character, a reputation that would command respect both at home and abroad. And in his conduct of the presidency Washington bent his every effort toward that end.[32]

He recognized that he was on trial, that the character of the government and the respect accorded it would be measured by the respect that he himself demanded and commanded. As president of a republic he aimed at an elegant simplicity in his style of living, sumptuous enough to escape any imputation of ostentatious poverty, but restrained enough to avoid outright splendor.[33] At the same time he cultivated his characteristic aloofness, even to the point where his critics charged that his condescension smacked of monarchy. And when rebellion broke out against taxes imposed by Congress, he responded with a vigor calculated to demonstrate that the new government would tolerate none of what Daniel Shays had tried in Massachusetts.

Washington identified the national interest so closely and so personally with the new national government that he could scarcely recognize the validity of any kind of dissent. It is all too easy at the present day to see his impatience with public criticism as intolerance bordering on paranoia. But Washington had borne the brunt of a war that was needlessly prolonged because of the supineness of the central government. He had watched the nation ap-

21

proach the point of dissolution in the 1780s, a development that threatened everything he had fought for. And in the 1790s it was by no means clear that the new government was there to stay. If he greeted criticism with distrust, it was because domestic dissent might belie the character he was seeking to establish for his government, might return the nation to the impotence of the 1780s, might signal to the watching world the predicted collapse of the republic.[34]

In spite of his determination to establish a strong character for the nation, Washington had no yearning for personal power, nor did he want any military adventures of the kind that so often infatuate men who are obsessed with power for its own sake. He did want the United States to grow in strength, for strength must be the ultimate basis of respect. And strength, he was sure, would not come to the United States by going to war. He had had ample experience that war was the way to poverty, and poverty meant impotence. The way for the country to grow strong, he believed, was to eschew internal dissension and steer clear of the quarrels which he saw were about to envelop the nations of Europe. The United States was encumbered with a French alliance, but as Washington read the terms of it, it did not require the United States to become involved in any quarrel that France might have with other countries, including England. And while he was grateful for the assistance received from France in the winning of American independence, he did not think that gratitude had a place in the determination of national policy. As he had pointed out some years earlier to Henry Laurens, the nation, like other nations, should not be counted on to act beyond its own interest. France in helping Americans during the Revolution had acted out of self interest — her interest to have England weakened by loss of the colonies. Now, as Washington saw it, the main interest of the United

States was to recover from the economic exhaustion incurred, however needlessly, in the Revolutionary War. The means of recovery, he thought, lay in exploiting the American land to produce as much as possible for sale to nations less fruitfully engaged in quarreling with one another. For this purpose it should welcome immigrants who tired of the heavy taxes that European governments imposed in order to maintain the splendor of their kings and the power of their armies. In America, now that a government existed capable of protecting life, liberty, and property, the industrious and ambitious, the poor, the needy, and the oppressed from all over the world would swell the ranks of American producers, and the United States would grow in power as the oppressive governments of Europe declined.[35]

Washington had no difficulty in persuading the new Congress or the advisers whom he appointed to his cabinet that a policy of neutrality was the way to let the United States develop its powers. But his advisers never understood the operation of the policy as well as Washington did. Jefferson was bent on making a weapon of neutrality, on wringing concessions, especially from England, in return for American neutrality. Hamilton, on the other hand, was highly conciliatory in trying to restore commercial relations with England, and went almost past the limits of neutrality in his obsession with the ideological dangers presented by the French Revolution. Although Washington was closer to Hamilton than to Jefferson neither of the two men fully grasped the sophistication of their chief's policy for the nation.[36]

Washington realized that the people of the United States would benefit from high prices for their agricultural exports while European farmers were distracted by war. But other than this benefit, he did not propose to take advantage of the distress of any country in order to wring

23

concessions from it, because he was convinced that benefits thus obtained would not last. In 1791, when he was about to appoint Gouverneur Morris (him of the slap on the back) as minister to France, he warned him against seeking to obtain favorable treaties from countries in distress, "for unless," he said, "treaties are mutually beneficial to the Parties, it is in vain to hope for a continuance of them beyond the moment when the one which conceives itself to be over-reached is in a situation to break off the connexion."[37] A treaty had to match the powers and interests of the parties making it. Otherwise it would be indeed a scrap of paper. Washington signed two treaties as president of the United States. The first one, Jay's Treaty with England, was extremely unpopular; and Washington himself did not think well of it. But he signed it because he thought that commercial relations with England would be worse with no treaty than with this one. The popular outcry against it did not move him and indeed struck him as senseless, because he believed that the United States in 1795 was not sufficiently powerful and England was not sufficiently weak to have negotiated a better treaty. And even if Jay had been able to get a better treaty than he had obtained, there was no reason to suppose that it would have been better kept than the peace treaty, in which England had agreed to give up her posts in the Northwest Territory. The fact that England had not yet given up the posts and that Jay had secured little more than another agreement for her to give them up was no surprise to Washington. The American negotiators at the peace conference had got more from England that America's bargaining powers really entitled her to. England's retention of the northwest posts was therefore to be expected. It would be foolish to reject Jay's Treaty if it might improve the commercial situation of the United States in any way.[38]

Washington could afford to be equally calm about

Pinckney's Treaty with Spain. That treaty was almost as popular with the American people as Jay's had been unpopular, and it has generally been hailed as a triumph because it secured the American right to navigate the Mississippi. Yet it merely obtained what Washington was certain the United States would get anyhow. After the Revolutionary War settlers had poured into the western country in such numbers that by 1795 Spain could not safely have denied them the right to export their produce down the Mississippi. What prompted the concession was not Pinckney's negotiating skill but the expanding American strength in the west and the strong character that Washington had conferred on the national government. Treaties, in Washington's view, were not important. What was important was power.[39]

Washington was not a man of many talents. He had none of the range of the brilliant men around him, the intellectual curiosity of a Jefferson, the fiscal genius of a Hamilton. But in his understanding of power he left them all behind, as he did the British generals who opposed him and the French who assisted him. When he retired from the presidency after eight years, he had placed the United States on the way to achieving the power that he had aspired to for it. In the years that have followed, that power has grown until there are those who wonder whether it has been a good thing for the world. But at the time it looked like a very good thing indeed. And for better or for worse, it was the work of George Washington, the man who still keeps us all at a distance.

GEORGE
WASHINGTON'S
VIRGINIA

Allegheny R.

Ft. Duquesne

Steubenville

• Johns

Ft. Henry

PENNS

Ohio R.

Monongahela R.

HAMPS

FRE

N

Cheat R.

VIR

Greenbrier R.

Jackson R.

• Harris

AUGUSTA

New R.

Ft. Dinwiddie

Miller's

• Augusta Co

Hot Springs

ALBE

Ft Dickinson

Catawba Cr.

Ft. William

Lynchburg

Ft.

Big Lick

Vass's Ft.

Vaux

(Roanoke)

• Charl

HALIFAX

Smith R.

Ft. Trial

Halifax •

Roan

Dan R.

A·Karl/J·Kemp

George Washington learned to write the way soldiers learn. Military officers in the eighteenth century, as in the twentieth, had to spend more time writing letters, even when at war, than in commanding troops. They wrote not simply because their superiors required it, but because it was the only way of getting the men and supplies and political support that they needed. In Washington's letters and dispatches we can follow the growth of his understanding of power, both military and political. The letters and extracts of letters that follow are samples selected for that purpose.

I

Washington's military career began at the age of twenty-one when Governor Robert Dinwiddie of Virginia sent him to the Ohio country with a message to the French there, inviting them to clear out. Since the French did not accept the invitation, Dinwiddie ordered Washington back the next year to build a fort at the present site of Pittsburgh. Arriving over the mountains, Washington discovered that the French had beaten him to it and were already at work on their own fort (Fort Duquesne). Not altogether wisely, he attacked a contingent of them in a skirmish that opened the French and Indian War, sometimes called the Great War for the Empire.

In 1755 he was back again as aide-de-camp to the unfortunate English general, Edward Braddock, in the latter's unsuccessful expedition against the French fort. After Braddock's failure opened Virginia's western frontier to French and Indian attack, Governor Dinwiddie appointed Washington, now twenty-three years old, as Colonel and Commander-in-Chief, to organize Virginia's defenses. By October, 1755, we find him in this position writing dispatches to the governor, pleading for the powers needed to carry out his mission.[1]

I wou'd again hint the necessity of putting the Militia

under a better Regulation; had I not mention'd it twice before, and a third time may seem Impertinent; but I must once more beg leave to declare, (for here I am more immediately concern'd), that unless the Assembly will Enact a Law, to enforce the Military Law in all its Parts, that I must, with great regret, decline the Honour that has been so generously intended me;[2] and for this only Reason I do it,—the foreknowledge I have of failing in every point that might justly be expected, from a person invested with full power to exert his Authority. I see the growing Insolence of the Soldiers, the Indolence and Inactivity of the Officers; who are all sensible how confined their punishments are, in regard to what they ought to be. In fine, I can plainly see, that under our present Establishment, we shall become a Nusance, and insupportable charge to our Country, and never answer any one expectation of the Assembly. And here, I must assume the Freedom to express some surprize, that we alone, should be so tenacious of our Liberty, as not to invest a power, where Interest and Politicks so unanswerably demand it; and from whence so much good must consequently ensue; do we not see that every Nation under the Sun find their account therein; and without, it no Order no regularity can be observed? Why then shou'd it be expected from us, (who are all young and inexperienced,) to govern, and keep up a proper spirit of Discipline with't Laws; when the best, and most Experienced, can scarcely do it with. Then if we consult our Interest, I am sure it is loudly called for. For I can confidently assert, that Recruiting, · Cloathing, Arming, Maintaining, and Subsisting Soldiers, who have deserted; has cost the Country an immense Sum, which might have been prevented, were we under Restraints, that would terrify the Soldiers from such practices. One thing more on this head I will recommend, and then quit the Subject; *i.e.,* to have the Inhabitants liable to certain heavy Fines or Corporal Punishments, for Entertaining of Deserters, and a Reward for taking them up. If this was done, it would be next to an impossibility for a Soldier to Escape; but, on the contrary, as things now stand, they are not only Seduced to run away, but are also harbour'd, and assisted with every necessary means to make their escape.

1. *Writings,* Fitzpatrick, ed., I, 202-203. All selections are from this source.
2. Washington writes as though he had not yet accepted command, but he had done so two months earlier. What he seems to be threatening here is a resignation.

II

Washington got his "Military Law," providing court-martial for deserters, but his troubles with militiamen never ended. A little over a year later he reported to Dinwiddie again, after a tour of Virginia's southwestern outposts.[1]

Honble. Sir: In mine from Halifax [County] I promised your Honor a particular detail of my remarks and observations upon the situation of our frontiers, when I arrived at this place.[2] Although I was pretty explicit in my former, I cannot avoid recapitulating part of the subject *now,* as my duty, and its importance for redress are strong motives.

From Fort Trial on Smith's River, I returned to Fort William on the Catawba, where I met Colonel Buchanan with about thirty men, (chiefly officers,) to conduct me up Jackson's River, along the range of forts. With this small company of irregulars, with whom order, regularity, circumspection, and vigilance were matters of derision and contempt, we set out, and, by the protection of Providence, reached Augusta Court-House in seven days, without meeting the enemy; otherwise we must have fallen a sacrifice, through the indiscretion of these whooping, hallooing *gentlemen* soldiers!

This jaunt afforded me an opportunity of seeing the bad regulation of the militia, the disorderly proceedings of the garrisons, and the unhappy circumstances of the inhabitants.

First, of the militia. The difficulty of collecting them upon any emergency whatever, I have often spoken of as grevious; and I appeal to sad experience, both in this and other countries, how great a disadvantage it is; the enemy having every opportunity to plunder, kill, and escape, before they can afford any assistance. And not to mention the expensiveness of their service in general, I can instance several cases, where a captain, lieutenant, and, I may add, an ensign, with two or three sergeants, and six or eight men, will go upon duty at a time. The proportion of expense in this case is so unjust and obvious, your Honor wants not to be proved.

Then these men, when raised, are to be continued only one month on duty, half of which time is lost in their marching out and home, (especially those from the adjacent counties,) who must be on duty some time before they reach their stations; by which means double sets of men are in pay at the same time, and for the same service. Again, the waste of provision they make is unaccountable; no method or order in being served or purchasing at the best rates, but quite the reverse. Allowance for each man, as other soldiers do, they look upon as the highest indignity, and would *sooner* starve, than carry a few days' provision on their backs for conveniency. But upon their march, when breakfast is wanted, knock down the first beef, &c, they meet with, and, after regaling themselves, march on until dinner, when they take the same method, and so for supper likewise, to the great oppression of the people. Or, if they chance to impress cattle for provision, the valuation is left to ignorant and indifferent neighbours, who have suffered by those practices, and, despairing of their pay, exact high prices, and thus the public is imposed on at all events. I might add, I believe, that, for the want of proper laws to govern the militia by (for I cannot ascribe it to any other cause), they are obstinate, self-willed, perverse, of little or no service to the people, and very burthensome to the country. Every *mean* individual has his own crude notions of things, and must undertake to direct. If his advice is neglected, he thinks himself slighted, abased, and injured; and, to redress his wrongs, will depart for his home. These, Sir, are literally matters of fact, partly from persons of undoubted veracity, but chiefly from my own observations.

Secondly, concerning the garrisons. I found them very weak for want of men; but more so by indolence and irregularity. None I saw in a posture of defence, and few that might not be surprised with the greatest ease. An instance of this appeared at Dickinson's Fort, where the Indians ran down, caught several children playing under the walls, and had got to the gate before they were discovered. Was not Vass's Fort surprised, and a good many souls lost, in the same manner? They keep no guard, but just when the enemy is about; and are under fearful apprehensions of them; nor ever stir out of the forts, from the time they reach them, till relieved on their month being expired; at which time they march off, be the event what it will. So that the neighbourhood may be ravaged by the enemy, and they not the wiser. Of the ammunition they are as careless as of the provisions, firing it away frequently at targets for wagers. On our journey, as we approached one of their forts, we heard a quick fire for several minutes, and concluded for certain that they were attacked; so we marched in the best manner to their relief; but when we came up, we found they were diverting at marks. These men afford no assistance to the unhappy settlers, who are drove from their plantations, either in securing their harvests, or gathering in their corn. Lieutenant Bullet, commanding at Fort Dinwiddie, sent to Major Lewis of Albemarle, who commanded a party of sixty militia at Miller's, about fifteen miles above him, where were also thirty men of Augusta, for some men to join his small parties to gather the corn. Major Lewis refused assistance, and would not divide his men. I wrote to him, but got no answer. Mr. Bullet has done what he could with his few; not quite thirty. Of the many forts, which I passed by, I saw but one or two that had their captains present, they being absent chiefly on their own business, and had given leave to several of the men to do the same. Yet these persons, I will venture to say, will charge the country their full month's pay.

Thirdly, the wretched and unhappy situation of the inhabitants needs few words, after a slight reflection on the preceding circumstances, which must certainly draw after them very melancholy consequences without speedy redress. They are truly sensible of their misery; they feel their insecurity from militia preservation, who are slow in coming to their assistance, indifferent about their preservation, unwilling to continue, and regardless of every thing but their own ease. In short, they are so affected with approaching ruin, that the whole back country is in a general motion towards the southern colonies; and I expect that scarce a family will inhabit Frederick, Hampshire, or Augusta, in a little time. They petitioned me in the most earnest manner for companies of the regiment. But alas! it is not in my power to assist them with any, except I leave this dangerous quarter more exposed than they are. I promised, at their particular request, to address your Honor and the Assembly in their behalf, and that a regular force may be established in lieu of the militia and ranging companies, which are of much less service, and infinitely more cost to the country. Were this done, the whole would be under one direction, and any misbehaviour could never pass with impunity. Whereas the others are soldiers at will, and in fact will go and come when and where they please, without regarding the orders or directions of any. And, indeed, the manner in which some of the ranging captains have obtained their commissions, if I am rightly informed, is by imposture and artifice. They produce a list, I am told, to your Honor, of sundry persons, who are willing to serve under them. One part, it is said, are of fictitious names; another, the names of persons who never saw the list; and the remainder are persons drawn into it by fallacious promises, that cannot be complied with without detriment to the service. But were it otherwise, surely any person, who considers the pay of the soldiers and that of the militia, will find a considerable difference, tho' both under the best regulations.

As defensive measures are evidently insufficient for the security and safety of the country, I hope no arguments are requisite to convince of the necessity of altering them to a vigorous offensive war, in order to remove the cause.

1. *Writings,* I, 492-96.
2. Winchester.

III

Washington's military experience on the Virginia frontier was one long series of frustrations, culminating in another expedition that captured Fort Duquesne only after the French had abandoned it. Following the French withdrawal, Washington settled down at Mt. Vernon and did not further cultivate his understanding of power until the quarrel with England over Parliamentary taxation obliged him to. As early as April, 1769, in a letter to his friend and neighbor George Mason, he considered the possibility of an ultimate recourse to arms, but favored first an attempt to bring the British to terms by a concerted boycott of their manufactures.[1]

At a time when our lordly Masters in Great Britain will be satisfied with nothing less than the deprication of American freedom, it seems highly necessary that some thing shou'd be done to avert the stroke and maintain the liberty which we have derived from our Ancestors; but the manner of doing it to answer the purpose effectually is the point in question.

That no man shou'd scruple, or hesitate a moment to use a-ms in defence of so valuable a blessing, on which all the good and evil of life depends; is clearly my opinion; yet A-ms I wou'd beg leave to add, should be the last resource; the denier resort. Addresses to the Throne, and remonstrances to parliament, we have already, it is said, proved the inefficacy of; how far then their attention to our rights and priviledges is to be awakened or alarmed by starving their Trade and manufactures, remains to be tryed.

The northern Colonies, it appears, are endeavouring to adopt this scheme. In my opinion it is a good one, and must be attended with salutary effects, provided it can be carried pretty generally into execution; but how far it is practicable to do so, I will not take upon me to determine. That there will be difficulties attending the execution of it every where, from clashing interests, and selfish designing men (ever attentive to their own gain, and watchful of every turn that can assist their lucrative views, in preference to any other consideration) cannot be denied; but in the Tobacco Colonies where the Trade is so diffused, and in a manner wholly conducted by Factors for their principals at home, these difficulties are certainly enhanced, but I think not insurmountably increased, if the Gentlemen in their several Counties wou'd be at some pains to explain matters to the people, and stimulate them to a cordial agreement to purchase none but certain innumerated Articles out of any of the Stores after such a period, not import nor purchase any themselves. This, if it did not effectually withdraw the Factors from their Importations, wou'd at least make them extremely cautious in doing it, as the prohibited Goods could be vended to none but the non-associator, or those who wou'd pay no regard to their association; both of whom ought to be stigmatized, and made the objects of publick reproach.

The more I consider a Scheme of this sort, the more ardently I wish success to it, because I think there are private, as well as public advantages to result from it; the former certain, however precarious the other may prove; for in respect to the latter I have always thought that by virtue of the same power (for here alone the authority derives) which assume's the right of Taxation, they may attempt at least to restrain our manufactories; especially those of a public.nature; the same equity and justice prevailing in the one case as the other, it being no greater hardship to forbid my manufacturing, than it is to order me to buy Goods of them loaded with Duties, for the express purpose of raising a revenue. But as a measure of this sort will be an additional exertion of arbitrary power, we cannot be worsted I think in putting it to the Test. On the other hand, that the Colonies are considerably indebted to Great Britain, is a truth universally acknowledged. That many families are reduced, almost, if not quite, to penury and want, from the low ebb of their fortunes, and Estates daily selling for the discharge of Debts, the public papers furnish but too many melancholy proofs of. And that a scheme of this sort will contribute more effectually than any other I can devise to immerge the Country from the distress it at present labours under, I do most firmly believe, if it can be generally adopted. And I can see but one set of people (the Merchants excepted) who will not, or ought not, to wish well to the Scheme; and that is those who live genteely and hospitably, on clear Estates. Such as these were they, not to consider the valuable object in view, and the good of others, might think it hard to be curtail'd in their living and enjoyments; for as to the penurious Man, he saves his money, and he saves his credit, having the best plea for doing that, which before perhaps he had the most violent struggles to refrain from doing. The extravagant and expensive man has the same good plea to retrench his Expences. He is thereby furnished with a pretext to live within bounds, and embraces it, prudence dictated oeconomy to him before, but his resolution was too weak to put in practice; for how can I, *says he,* who have lived in such and such a manner change my method? I am ashamed to do it; and besides such an alteration in the system of my living, will create suspicions of a decay in my fortune, and such a thought the World must not harbour; I will e'en continue my course: till at last the course discontinues the Estate, a sale of it being the consequence of his perseverance in error. This I am satisfied is the way that many who have set out in the wrong tract, have reasoned, till ruin stares them in the face. And in respect to the poor and needy man, he is only left in the same situation he was found; better I might say, because as he judges from comparison his condition is amended in proportion as it approaches nearer to those above him.

Upon the whole therefore, I think the Scheme a good one, and that it ought to be tryed here, with such alterations as the exigency of our circumstances render absolutely necessary; but how, and in what manner to begin the work, is a matter worthy of consideration, and whether it can be attempted with propriety, or efficacy (further than a communication of sentiments to one another) before May, when the Court and Assembly will meet together in Williamsburg, and a uniform plan can be concerted, and sent into the different counties to operate at the same time, and in the same manner every where, is a thing I am somewhat in doubt upon, and shou'd be glad to know your opinion of. I am Dr. Sir, etc.

---

1. *Writings,* II, 500-504.

IV

The non-importation agreements did bring results in repeal of most of the Parliamentary taxes in 1770. But the quarrel erupted again in 1773 with the Tea Act and the famous Boston Tea Party. When England responded to the Tea Party with the punitive Coercive Acts against Massachusetts, Washington, along with most other Virginia gentlemen, was persuaded that only a firm and united stand by all the colonies could prevent Parliament and the ministry from destroying American rights. His good friend Bryan Fairfax preferred petitions. In July, 1774 Washington explained to Fairfax why in his view the time had come for petitions to give way to power.[1]

That I differ very widely from you, in respect to the mode of obtaining a defeat [repeal] of the acts so much and so justly complained of, I shall not hesitate to acknowledge; and that this difference in opinion may probably proceed from the different constructions we put upon the conduct and intention of the ministry may also be true; but, as I see nothing, on the one hand, to induce a belief that the Parliament would embrace a favorable opportunity of repealing acts, which they go on with great rapidity to pass, and in order to enforce their tyrannical system; and, on the other, I observe, or think I observe, that government is pursuing a regular plan at the expense of law and justice to overthrow our constitutional rights and liberties, how can I expect any redress from a measure, which has been ineffectually tried already? For, Sir, what is it we are contending against? Is it against paying the duty of three pence per pound on tea because burthensome? No, it is the right only, we have all along disputed, and to this end we have already petitioned his Majesty in as humble and dutiful manner as subjects could do. Nay, more, we applied to the House of Lords and House of Commons in their different legislative capacities, setting forth, that, as Englishmen, we could not be deprived of this essential and valuable part of a constitution. If, then, as the fact really is, it is against the right of taxation that we now do, and, (as I before said,) all along have contended, why should they suppose an exertion of this power would be less obnoxious now than formerly? And what reasons have we to believe, that they would make a second attempt, while the same sentiments filled the breast of every American, if they did not intend to enforce it if possible?

The conduct of the Boston people could not justify the rigor of their measures, unless there had been a requisition of payment and refusal of it; nor did that measure require an act to deprive the government of Massachusetts Bay of their charter, or to exempt offenders from trial in the place where offences were committed, as there was not, nor could not be, a single instance produced to manifest the necessity of it. Are not all these things self evident proofs of a fixed and uniform plan to tax us? If we want further proofs, do not all the debates in the House of Commons serve to confirm this? And has not General Gage's conduct since his arrival,[2] (in stopping the address of his Council, and publishing a proclamation more becoming a Turkish bashaw, than an English governor, declaring it treason to associate in any manner by which the commerce of Great Britain is to be affected,) exhibited an unexampled testimony of the most despotic system of tyranny, that ever was practised in a free government? In short, what further proofs are wanted to satisfy one of the designs of the ministry, than their own acts, which are uniform and plainly tending to the same point, nay, if I mistake not, avowedly to fix the right of taxation? What hope then from petitioning, when they tell us, that now or never is the time to fix the matter? Shall we, after this, whine and cry for relief, when we have already tried it in vain? Or shall we supinely sit and see one province after another fall a prey to despotism? If I was in any doubt, as to the right which the Parliament of Great Britain had to tax us without our consent, I should most heartily coincide with you in opinion, that to petition, and petition only, is the proper method to apply for relief; because we should then be asking a favor, and not claiming a right, which, by the law of nature and our constitution, we are, in my opinion, indubitably entitled to. I should even think it criminal to go further than this, under such an idea; but none such I have. I think the Parliament of Great Britain hath no more right to put their hands into my pocket, without my consent, than I have to put my hands into yours for money; and this being already urged to them in a firm, but decent manner, by all the colonies, what reason is there to expect any thing from their justice?

1. *Writings,* III, 231-34.
2. General Thomas Gage arrived in Boston on May 17, 1774, commissioned both as Governor of Massachusetts and as Commander in Chief of British forces in North America.

V

Washington was right. The First Continental Congress, which met in the fall of 1774, did petition, but to no avail. When the second Congress met in May, 1775, with Washington (as at the first Congress) a delegate from Virginia, war had already begun, and Congress appointed Washington as Commander-in-Chief of a Continental Army to carry it on. At the time when Washington accepted command, his army did not yet exist. Boston was under siege by the militiamen who had routed the British from Lexington and Concord on April 19. The initial success of the New England militia on that day and their formidable performance two months later at Bunker Hill gave Americans a confidence in their ability to defeat the British in a quick, easy war. The Continental Congress thought it would be sufficient to enlist men in the Continental Army for short terms. Washington's assessment of British power and American prowess was different. After his experience with short-term militiamen in the previous war against the French, he wanted an army that he could train and discipline for the formidable contest he saw in the offing. Washington's opinions were confirmed by the failure in the winter of 1775-76 of the expedition undertaken against Quebec under General Richard Montgomery. In a letter to his former secretary, Joseph Reed, on February 1, 1776, Washington explained his views succinctly.[1]

> The account given of the behavior of the men under General Montgomery, is exactly consonant to the opinion I have formed of these people, and such as they will exhibit abundant proofs of, in similar cases whenever called upon. Place them behind a parapet a breastwork, stone wall, or any thing that will afford them shelter, and, from their knowledge of a firelock, they will give a good account of their enemy; but I am as well convinced, as if I had seen it, that they will not march boldly up to a work, nor stand exposed in a plain; and yet, if we are furnished with the means, and the weather will afford us a passage, and we can get in men, (for these three things are necessary,) something must be attempted. The men must be brought to face danger; they cannot always have an intrenchment or a stone wall as a safeguard or shield; and it is of essential importance, that the troops in

42

Boston should be destroyed if possible before they can be reinforced or removed. This is clearly my opinion. Whether circumstances will admit of the trial, and, if tried, what will be the event, the all-wise Disposer of them alone can tell.

The evils arising from short, or even any limited enlistment of the troops, are greater, and more extensively hurtful than any person (not an eye-witness to them) can form any idea of. It takes you two or three months to bring new men in any tolerable degree acquainted with their duty; it takes a longer time to bring a people of the temper and genius of these into such a subordinate way of thinking as is necessary for a soldier, before this is accomplished, the time approaches for their dismissal, and you are beginning to make interest for their continuance for another limited period; in the doing of which you are obliged to relax in your discipline, in order as it were to curry favour with them, by which means the latter part of your time is employed in undoing what the first was accomplishing, and instead of having men always ready to take advantage of circumstances, you must govern your movements by the circumstances of your enlistment. This is not all; by the time you have got men armed and equipped, the difficulty of doing which is beyond description, and with every new set you have the same trouble to encounter, without the means of doing it. — in short, the disadvantages are so great and apparent to me, that I am convinced, uncertain as the continuance of the war is, that Congress had better determine to give a bounty of 20, 30, or even 40 Dollars to every man who will Inlist for the whole time, be it long or short. I intend to write my sentiments fully on this subject to Congress the first leisure time I have.

1. *Writings,* IV, 299-300.

VI

Washington wrote to Congress, but he never got the number of men he needed on long term enlistments, and for the rest of the war Washington had to give the major part of his energy simply to keeping his army in existence. On September 24, 1776, he wrote from Harlem Heights to the President of Congress, John Hancock, a letter typical of those he was to address to Congress for many more months and years than he could have foreseen at the time.[1]

> Sir: From the hours allotted to Sleep, I will borrow a few Moments to convey my thoughts on sundry important matters to Congress. I shall offer them, with that sincerity which ought to characterize a man of candour; and with the freedom which may be used in giving useful information, without incurring the imputation of presumption.
>
> We are now as it were, upon the eve of another dissolution of our Army; the remembrance of the difficulties which happened upon that occasion last year, the consequences which might have followed the change, if proper advantages had been taken by the Enemy; added to a knowledge of the present temper and Situation of the Troops, reflect but a very gloomy prospect upon the appearance of things now, and satisfie me, beyond the possibility of doubt, that unless some speedy, and effectual measures are adopted by Congress, our cause will be lost.
>
> It is in vain to expect, that any (or more than a trifling) part of this Army will again engage in the Service on the encouragement offered by Congress. When Men find that their Townsmen and Companions are receiving 20, 30, and more Dollars, for a few Months Service, (which is truely the case) it cannot be expected;[2] without using compulsion; and to force

them into the Service would answer no valuable purpose. When Men are irritated, and the Passions inflamed, they fly hastely and chearfully to Arms; but after the first emotions are over, to expect, among such People, as compose the bulk of an Army, that they are influenced by any other principles than those of Interest, is to look for what never did, and I fear never will happen; the Congress will deceive themselves therefore if they expect it.

A Soldier reasoned with upon the goodness of the cause he is engaged in, and the inestimable rights he is contending for, hears you with patience, and acknowledges the truth of your observations, but adds, that it is of no more Importance to him than others. The Officer makes you the same reply, with this further remark, that his pay will not support him, and he cannot ruin himself and Family to serve his Country, when every Member of the community is equally Interested and benefitted by his Labours. The few therefore, who act upon Principles of disinterestedness, are, comparatively speaking, no more than a drop in the Ocean. It becomes evidently clear then, that as this Contest is not likely to be the Work of a day; as the War must be carried on systematically, and to do it, you must have good Officers, there are, in my Judgment, no other possible means to obtain them but by establishing your Army upon a permanent footing; and giving your Officers good pay; this will induce Gentlemen, and Men of Character to engage; and till the bulk of your Officers are composed of such persons as are actuated by Principles of honour, and a spirit of enterprize, you have little to expect from them. — They ought to have such allowances as will enable them to live like, and support the Characters of Gentlemen; and not be driven by a scanty pittance to the low, and dirty arts which many of them practice, to filch the Public of more than the difference of pay would amount to upon an ample allowe. besides, something is due to the Man who puts his life in his hands, hazards his health, and forsakes the Sweets of domestic enjoyments. Why a Captn. in the Continental Service should receive no more than 5/.Currency per day, for performing the same duties that an officer of the same Rank in the British Service receives 10/. Sterlg. for, I never could conceive; especially when the latter is provided with every necessary he requires, upon the best terms, and the former can scarce procure them, at any Rate. There is nothing that gives a Man consequence, and renders him fit for Command, like a support that renders him Independant of every body but the State he Serves.

With respect to the Men, nothing but a good bounty can obtain them upon a permanent establishment; and for no shorter time than the continuance of the War, ought they to be engaged; as Facts incontestibly prove, that the difficulty, and cost of Inlistments, increase with time. When the Army was first raised at Cambridge, I am persuaded the Men might have been got without a bounty for the War: after this, they began to see that the Contest was not likely to end so speedily as was immagined, and to feel their consequence, by remarking, that to get the Militia In, in the course of last year, many Towns were induced to give them a bounty. Foreseeing the Evils resulting from this, and the destructive consequences which unavoidably would follow short Inlistments, I took the Liberty in a long Letter, written by myself (date not now recollected, as my Letter Book is not here) to recommend the Inlistments for and during the War; assigning such Reasons for it, as experience has since convinced me were well founded. At that time twenty Dollars would, I am persuaded, have engaged the Men for this term. But it will not do to look back, and if the present opportunity is slip'd, I am perswaded that twelve months more will Increase our difficulties fourfold. I shall therefore take the freedom of giving it as my opinion, that a good Bounty be immediately offered, aided by the proffer of at least 100, or 150 Acres of Land and a suit of Cloaths and Blankt, to each non-Comd. Officer and Soldier; as I have good authority for saying, that however high the Men's pay may appear, it is barely sufficient in the present scarcity and dearness of all kinds of goods, to keep them in Cloaths, much less afford support to their Families. If this encouragement then is given to the Men, and such Pay allowed the Officers as will induce Gentlemen of Character and liberal Sentiments to engage; and proper care and precaution are used in the nomination (having more regard to the Characters of Persons, than the Number of Men they can Inlist) we should in a little time have an Army able to cope with any that can be opposed to it, as there are excellent Materials to form one out of: but while the only merit an Officer possesses is his ability to raise Men; while those Men consider, and treat him as an equal; and (in the Character of an Officer) regard him no more than a broomstick, being mixed together as one common herd; no order, nor no discipline can prevail; nor will the Officer ever meet with that respect which is essentially necessary to due subordination.

To place any dependance upon Militia, is, assuredly, resting upon a broken staff. Men just dragged from the tender Scenes fo domestick life; unaccustomed to the din of Arms; totally unacquainted with every kind of Military skill, which being followed by a want of confidence in themselves, when opposed to Troops regularly train'd, disciplined, and appointed, superior in knowledge, and superior in Arms, makes them timid, and ready to fly from their own shadows. Besides, the sudden change in their manner of living, (particularly in the lodging) brings on sickness in many; impatience in all, and such an unconquerable desire of returning to their respective homes that it not only produces shameful, and scandalous Desertions among themselves, but infuses the like spirit in others. Again, Men accustomed to unbounded freedom, and no controul, cannot brook the Restraint which is indispensably necessary to the good order and Government of an Army; without which, licentiousness, and every kind of disorder triumpantly reign. To bring Men to a proper degree of Subordination, is not the work of a day, a Month or even a year; and unhappily for us, and the cause we are Engaged in, the little discipline I have been labouring to establish in the Army under my immediate Command, is in a manner done away by having such a mixture of Troops as have been called together within these few Months.

Relaxed, and unfit, as our Rules and Regulations of War are, for the Government of an Army, the Militia (those properly so called, for of these we have two sorts, the Six Months Men and those sent in as a temporary aid) do not think themselves subject to 'em, and therefore take liberties, which the Soldier is punished for; this creates jealousy; jealousy begets dissatisfaction, and these by degrees ripen into Mutiny; keeping the whole Army in a confused, and disordered State; rendering the time of those who wish to see regularity and good Order prevail more unhappy than Words can describe. Besides this, such repeated changes take place, that all arrangement is set at nought, and the constant fluctuation of things, deranges every plan, as fast as adopted.

These Sir, Congress may be assured, are but a small part of the Inconveniences which might be enumerated and attributed to Militia; but there is one that merits particular attention, and that is the expence. Certain I am, that it would be cheaper to keep 50, or 100,000 Men in constant pay than to depend upon half the number, and supply the other half occasionally by Militia. The time the latter is in pay before and after they are in Camp, assembling and Marching; the waste of Ammunition; the consumption of Stores, which in spite of every Resolution, and requisition of Congress they must be furnished with, or sent home, added to other incidental expences consequent upon their coming, and conduct in Camp, surpasses all Idea, and destroys every kind of regularity and oeconomy which you could establish among fixed and Settled Troops; and will, in my opinion prove (if the scheme is adhered to) the Ruin of our Cause.

The Jealousies of a standing Army, and the Evils to be apprehended from one, are remote; and in my judgment, situated and circumstanced as we are, not at all to be dreaded; but the consequence of wanting one, according to my Ideas, formed from the present view of things, is certain, and inevitable Ruin; for if I was called upon to declare upon Oath, whether the Militia have been most serviceable or hurtful upon the whole; I should subscribe to the latter. I do not mean by this however to arraign the Conduct of Congress, in so doing I should equally condemn my own measures, (if I did not my judgment); but experience, which is the best criterion to work by, so fully, clearly,

and decisively reprobates the practice of trusting to
Militia, that no Man who regards order, regularity,
and oeconomy; or who has any regard for his own
honour, Character, or peace of Mind, will risk them
upon this Issue.

1. *Writings*, VI, 106-112.
2. Washington refers to the practice adopted by some states of
   paying bounties for service in the militia at a higher rate
   than Congress was paying for enlistment in the Continental
   Army.

VII

As it became clear that Congress was failing to
mobilize effectively the resources of the country,
Washington worried that the people would become tired
of the war and succumb to offers of peace that fell short of
the recognition of American independence. In fact, on
April 12, 1778, England had already commissioned the
Earl of Carlisle to bring to the Americans a proposal that
agreed to virtually every pre-war American demand.
Washington suspected that something like this was in the
offing when he wrote on April 21 from Valley Forge to
John Bannister, a Virginia delegate to Congress.[1]

The difference between our service and that of the
Enemy, is very striking. With us, from the peculiar,
unhappy situation of things, the Officer, a few instances excepted, must break in upon his private
fortune for present support, without a prospect of
future relief. With them, even Companies are es-
teemed so honourable and so valuable, that they have
sold of late from 15 to 2,200 £ Sterling, and I am
credibly informed, that 4,000 Guineas have been

given for a Troop of Dragoons: You will readily determine how this difference will operate; what effects it must produce. Men may speculate as they will; they may talk of patriotism; they may draw a few examples from ancient story, of great atchievements performed by its influence; but whoever builds upon it, as a sufficient Basis for conducting a long and bloody War, will find themselves deceived in the end. We must take the passions of Men as Nature has given them, and those principles as a guide which are generally the rule of Action. I do not mean to exclude altogether the Idea of Patriotism. I know it exists, and I know it has done much in the present Contest. But I will venture to assert, that a great and lasting War can never be supported on this principle alone. It must be aided by a prospect of Interest or some reward. For a time, it may, of itself push Men to Action; to bear much, to encounter difficulties; but it will not endure unassisted by Interest.

The necessity of putting the Army upon a respectable footing, both as to numbers and constitution, is now become more essential than ever. The Enemy are beginning to play a Game more dangerous than their efforts by Arms, tho' these will not be remitted in the smallest degree, and which threatens a fatal blow to American Independence, and to her liberties of course: They are endeavouring to ensnare the people by specious allurements of Peace. It is not improbable they have had such abundant cause to be tired of the War, that they may be sincere, in the terms they offer, which, though far short of our pretensions, will be extremely flattering to Minds that do not penetrate far into political consequences: But, whether they are sincere or not, they may be equally destructive; for, to discerning Men, nothing can be more evident, than that a Peace on the principles of dependance, however limited, after what has happened, would be to the last degree dishonourable and ruinous. It is, however, much to be apprehended, that the Idea of such an event will have a very powerful effect upon the Country, and, if not combatted with the greatest address, will serve, at least, to produce supineness and dis-union. Men are naturally fond of Peace, and there are Symptoms which may authorize an Opinion, that the people of America are pretty generally weary of the present War. It is doubtful, whether many of our friends might not incline to an accommodation on the Grounds held out, or which may be, rather than persevere in a contest for Independence. If this is the case, it must surely be the truest policy to strengthen the Army, and place it upon a substantial footing. This will conduce to inspire the Country with confidence; enable those at the head of affairs to consult the public honour and interest, notwithstanding the defection of some and temporary inconsistency and irresolution of others, who may desire to compromise the dispute; and if a Treaty should be deemed expedient, will put it in their power to insist upon better terms, than they could otherwise expect.

Besides, the most vigorous exertions at Home, to increase and establish our Military force upon a good Basis; it appears to me advisable, that we should immediately try the full extent of our interest abroad and bring our European Negotiations to an Issue. I think France must have ratified our Independence, and will declare War immediately, on finding that serious proposals of accommodation are made; but lest, from a mistaken policy, or too exalted an Opinion of our powers, from the representations she has had, she should still remain indecisive, it were to be wished proper persons were instantly dispatched, or our envoys, already there, instructed, to insist pointedly on her coming to a final determination. It cannot be fairly supposed, that she will hesitate a moment to declare War, if she is given to understand, in a proper manner, that a reunion of the two Countries may be the consequence of procrastination. An European War, and an European Alliance would effectually answer our purposes. If the step I now mention, should be eligible, despatches ought to be sent at once, by different conveyances, for fear of accidents. I confess it appears to me, a measure of this kind could not but be productive of the most salutary consequences. If possible, I should also suppose it absolutely necessary, to obtain good intelligence from England, pointing out the true springs of this manoeuvre of Ministry; the preparations of force they are making; the prospects there are of raising it; the amount, and when it may be expected.

It really seems to me, from a comprehensive view of things, that a period is fast approaching, big with events of the most intersting importance. When the councils we pursue and the part we act, may lead decisively to liberty, or to Slavery. Under this Idea, I cannot but regret, that inactivity, that inattention, that want of something, which unhappily, I have but too often experienced in our public Affairs. I wish that our representation in Congress was compleat and full from every State, and that it was formed of the first Abilities among us. Whether we continue to War, or proceed to Negotiate, the Wisdom of America in Council cannot be too great. Our situation will be truly delicate. To enter into a Negotiation too hastily, or to reject it altogether, may be attended with consequences equally fatal. The wishes of the people, seldom founded in deep disquisitions, or resulting from other reasonings than their present feeling, may not intirely accord with our true policy and interest. If they do not, to observe a proper line of conduct, for promoting the one, and avoiding offence to the other, will be a Work of great difficulty. Nothing short of Independence, it appears to me, can possibly do. A Peace, on other terms, would, if I may be allowed the expression, be a Peace of War. The injuries we have received from the British Nation were so unprovoked; have been so great and so many, that they can never be forgotten. Besides the feuds, the jealousies; the animosities that would ever attend a Union with them. Besides the importance, the advantages we should derive from an unrestricted commerce; Our fidelity as a people; Our gratitude; Our Character as Men, are opposed to a coalition with them as subjects, but in case of the last extremity. Were we easily to accede to terms of dependence, no nation, upon future occasions, let the oppressions of Britain be never so flagrant and unjust, would interpose for our relief, or at least they would do it with a cautious reluctance and upon conditions, most probably, that would be hard, if not dishonourable to us. France, by her supplies, has saved us from the Yoke thus far, and a wise and virtuous perseverence, would and I trust will, free us entirely.

---

1. *Writings,* XI, 286-90.

VIII

France did acknowledge American independence, and Congress successfully resisted the blandishments of British peace offers. But as the war dragged on, Washington saw the strength of the country sapped not only by ineffective mobilization of manpower in sufficient quantity but also by a declining sense of nationality. American strength lay in union, and by 1778 the union formed so spontaneously in the Continental Congress of 1774 seemed to be giving way to petty bickering. In December, 1778, Washington wrote in distress to his friend and fellow Virginian, Benjamin Harrison.[1]

I can assign but two causes for the enemys continuance among us, and these balance so equally in my Mind, that I scarce know which of the two preponderates. The one is, that they are waiting the ultimate determination of Parliament; the other, that of our distresses; by which I know the Commissioners[2] went home not a little buoyed up; and sorry I am to add, not without cause. What may be the effect of such large and frequent emissions,[3] of the dissentions, Parties, extravagance, and a general lax of public virtue Heaven alone can tell! I am affraid even to think of It; but it appears as clear to me as ever the Sun did in its meredian brightness, that America never stood in more eminent need of the wise, patriotic, and Spirited exertions of her Sons than at this period and if it is not a sufficient cause for genl. lamentation, my misconception of the matter impresses it too strongly upon me, that the States seperately are too much engaged in their local concerns, and have too many of their ablest men withdrawn from the general Council for the good of the common weal; in a word, I think our political system may, be compared to the mechanism of a Clock; and that our conduct should derive a lesson from it for it answers no good purpose to keep the smaller Wheels in order if the greater one which is the support and prime mover of the whole is neglected. How far the latter is the case does not become me to pronounce but as there can be no harm in a pious wish for the good of ones Country I shall offer it as mine that each State wd. not only choose, but absolutely compel their ablest Men to attend Congress; that they would instruct them to go into a thorough investigation of the causes that have produced so many disagreeable effects in the Army and Country; in a word that public abuses should be corrected, and an entire reformation worked; without these it does not, in my judgment, require the spirit of divination to foretell the consequences of the present Administration, nor to how little purpose the States, individually, are framing constitutions, providing laws, and filling Offices with the abilities of their ablest Men. These, if the great whole is mismanaged must sink in the general wreck and will carry with it the remorse of thinking that we are lost by our own folly and negligence, or the desire perhaps of living in ease and tranquility during the expected accomplishment of so great a revolution in the effecting of which the greatest abilities and the honestest Men our (i. e. the American) world affords ought to be employed. It is much to be feared my dear Sir that the States in their seperate capacities have very inadequate ideas of the present danger. Removed (some of them) far distant from the scene of action and seeing, and hearing such publications only as flatter their wishes they conceive that the contest is at an end, and that to regulate the government and police of their own State is all that remains to be done; but it is devoutly to be wished that a sad reverse of this may not fall upon them like a thunder clap that is little expected. I do not mean to designate particular States. I wish to cast no reflections upon any one. The Public believes (and if they do believe it, the fact might almost as well be so) that the States at this time are badly represented, and that the great, and important concerns of the nation are horribly conducted, for want either of abilities or application in the Members, or through discord and party views of some individuals; that they should be so, is to be lamented more at this time, than formerly, as we are far advanced in the dispute and in the opinn. of many drawg. to a happy period; have the eyes of Europe upon us, and I am perswaded many political Spies to watch, discover our situation, and give information of our weaknesses and wants....

P.S. Phila. 30th. This Letter was to have gone by Post from Middle brook but missed that conveyance, since which I have come to this place at the request of Congress whence I shall soon return.

I have seen nothing since I came here (on the 22d. Instt.) to change my opinion of Men or Measrs. but abundant reason to be convinced, that our Affairs are in a more distressed, ruinous, and deplorable condition than they have been in Since the commencement of the War. By a faithful labourer then in the cause. By a Man who is daily injuring his private Estate without even the smallest earthly advantage not common to all in case of a favourable Issue to the dispute. By one who wishes the prosperity of America most devoutly and sees or thinks he sees it, on the brink of ruin, you are beseeched most earnestly my dear Colo. Harrison, to exert yourself in endeavouring to rescue your Country, by, (let me add) sending your ablest and best Men to Congress; these characters must not slumber, nor sleep at home, in such times of pressing danger; they must not content themselves in the enjoyment of places of honor or profit in their own Country, while the common interests of America are mouldering and sinking into irretrievable (if a remedy is not soon applied) ruin, in which theirs also must ultimately be involved. If I was to be called upon to draw A picture of the times, and of Men; from what I have seen, heard, and in part know I should in one word say that idleness, dissipation and extravagance seem to have laid fast hold of most of them. That Speculation, peculation, and an insatiable thirst for riches seems to have got the better of every other consideration and almost of every order of Men. That party disputes and personal quarrels are the great business of the day whilst the momentous concerns of an empire, a great and accumulated debt; ruined finances, depreciated money, and want of credit (which in their consequences is the want of every thing) are but secondary considerations and postponed from day to day, from week to week as if our affairs wore the most promising aspect; after drawing this picture, which from my Soul I believe to be a true one I need not repeat to you that I am alarmed and wish to see my Countrymen roused. I have no resentments, nor do I mean to point at any particular characters; this I can declare upon my honor for I have every attention paid me by Congress than I can possibly expect and have reason to think that I stand well in their estimation but in the present situation of things I cannot help asking: Where is Mason, Wythe, Jefferson, Nicholas, Pendleton, Nelson, and another I could name [George Mason, George Wythe, Thomas Jefferson, Wilson Cary

Nicholas, Edmund Pendleton, Thomas Nelson, jr., and Benjamin Harrison.]; and why, if you are sufficiently impressed with your danger, do you not (as New Yk. has done in the case of Mr. Jay) send an extra Member or two for at least a certain limited time till the great business of the Nation is put upon a more respectable and happy establishmt. Your Money is now sinking 5 pr. Ct. a day in this City; and I shall not be surprized if in the course of a few months a total stop is put to the currency of it. And yet an assembly, a concert, a Dinner, or Supper (that will cost three or four hundred pounds) will not only take Men of from acting in but even from thinking of this business while a great part of the Officers of your Army from absolute necessity are quitting the Service and the more virtuous few rather than do this are sinking by sure degrees into beggery and want. I again repeat to you that this is not an exaggerated acct.; that it is an alarming one I do not deny, and confess to you that I feel more real distress on acct. of the prest. appearances of things than I have done at any one time since the commencement of the dispute; but it is time to bid you once more adieu. Providence has heretofore taken us up when all other means and hope seemed to be departing from us, in this I will confide. Yr. &ca.

---

1. *Writings*, XIII, 463-68.
2. The British peace commission headed by the Earl of Carlisle (see above).
3. of paper money.

IX

The longer the war lasted, the more the weakening United States came to depend on foreign assistance. Washington was alert from the beginning to the dangers that this might involve, and he took special alarm at a proposal (made by the Marquis de Lafayette and warmly received in Congress) for an invasion of Canada by French troops. As already indicated above (p. 15), he wrote a lengthy argument against the expedition in an official communication to Congress, but on November 14, 1778 he dispatched a private letter to Henry Laurens, who had succeeded Hancock as President of Congress. No single letter in this collection better illustrates Washington's quick grasp of the realities of international power politics.[1]

Dear Sir: This will be accompanied by an official letter on the subject of the proposed expedition against Canada. You will perceive I have only considered it in a military light; indeed I was not authorised to consider it in any other; and I am not without apprehensions, that I may be thought, in what I have done, to have exceeded the limits intended by Congress. But my solicitude for the public welfare which I think deeply interested in this affair, will I hope justify me in the eyes of all those who view things through that just medium.

I do not know, Sir, what may be your sentiments in the present case; but whatever they are I am sure I can confide in your honor and friendship, and shall not hesitate to unbosom myself to you on a point of the most delicate and important Nature.

The question of the Canadian expedition in the form it now stands appears to me one of the most interesting that has hitherto agitated our National deliberations. I have one objection to it, untouched in my public letter, which is in my estimation, insurmountable, and alarms all my feelings for the true and permanent interests of my country. This is the introduction of a large body of French troops into Canada, and putting them in possession of the capital of that Province, attached to them by all the ties of blood, habits, manners, religion and former connexion of government. I fear this would be too great a temptation, to be resisted by any power actuated by the common maxims of national policy. Let us realize for a moment the striking advantages France would derive from the possession of Canada; the acquisition of an extensive territory abounding in supplies for the use of her Islands; the opening a vast source of the most beneficial commerce with the Indian nations, which she might then monopolize; the having ports of her own on this continent independent on the precarious good will of an ally; the engrossing the whole trade of New found land whenever she pleased, the finest nursery of seamen in the world; the security afforded to her Islands; and finally, the facility of awing and controuling these states, the natural and most formidable rival of every maritime power in Europe. Canada would be a solid acquisition to France on all these accounts and because of the numerous inhabitants, subjects to her by inclination, who would aid in preserving it under her power against the attempt of every other.

France acknowledged for some time past the most powerful monarchy in Europe by land, able now to dispute the empire of the sea with Great Britain, and if joined with Spain, I may say certainly superior, possessed of New Orleans, on our Right, Canada on our left and seconded by the numerous tribes of Indians on our Rear from one extremity to the other, a people, so generally friendly to her and whom she knows so well how to conciliate; would, it is much to be apprehended have it in her power to give law to these states.

Let us suppose, that when the five thousand french troops (and under the idea of that number twice as many might be introduced,) were entered the city of Quebec; they should declare an intention to hold Canada, as a pledge and surety for the debts due to France from the United States, or, under other specious pretences hold the place till they can find a bone for contention, and in the meanwhile should excite the Canadians to engage in supporting their pretences and claims; what should we be able to say with only four or five thousand men to carry on the dispute? It may be supposed that France would not choose to renounce our friendship by a step of this kind as the consequence would probably be a reunion with England on some terms or other; and the loss of what she had acquired, in so violent and unjustifiable a manner, with all the advantages of an Alliance with us. This in my opinion is too slender a security against the measure to be relied on. The truth of the position will intirely depend on naval events. If France and Spain should unite and obtain a decided superiority by Sea, a reunion with England would avail very little and might be set at defiance. France, with a numerous army at command might throw in what number of land forces she thought proper to support her pretensions; and England without men, without money, and inferior on her favourite element could give no effectual aid to oppose them. Resentment, reproaches, and submission seem to be all that would be left us. Men are very apt to run into extremes; hatred to England may carry some into an excess of Confidence in France; especially when motives of gratitude

62

are thrown into the scale. Men of this description would be unwilling to suppose France capable of acting so ungenerous a part. I am heartily disposed to entertain the most favourable sentiments of our new ally and to cherish them in others to a reasonable degree; but it is a maxim founded on the universal experience of mankind, that no nation is to be trusted farther than it is bound by its interest; and no prudent statesman or politician will venture to depart from it. In our circumstances we ought to be particularly cautious; for we have not yet attained sufficient vigor and maturity to recover from the shock of any false step into which we may unwarily fall.

If France should even engage in the scheme, in the first instance with the purest intentions, there is the greatest danger that, in the progress of the business, invited to it by circumstances and, perhaps, urged on by the solicitations and wishes of the Canadians, she would alter her views.

As the Marquis clothed his proposition when he spoke of it to me, it would seem to originate wholly with himself; but it is far from impossible that it had its birth in the Cabinet of France and was put into this artful dress, to give it the readier currency. I fancy that I read in the countenances of some people on this occasion, more than the disinterested zeal of allies. I hope I am mistaken and that my fears of mischief make me refine too much, and awaken jealousies that have no sufficient foundation.

But upon the whole, Sir, to wave every other consideration; I do not like to add to the number of our national obligations. I would wish as much as possible to avoid giving a foreign power new claims of merit for services performed, to the United States, and would ask no assistance that is not indispensible. I am, etc.

1. *Writings,* XIII, 254-57.

X

The expedition to Canada was averted, but American dependence on France continued — and continued to worry the Commander-in-Chief. The war had become an extension of the old contest between England and France, and Washington saw, as few of his contemporaries did, that the fate of the United States might depend on the differing resources that the two major powers could muster over the long pull. By 1780 it had become apparent that France, even with the aid of Spain, could achieve only a precarious superiority over Britain at sea. Recognizing the need for that superiority if *his* war was to be won, Washington gave a gloomy analysis of the situation in May, 1780, in a letter to his old secretary, Joseph Reed, now President of the Executive Council of Pennsylvania.[1]

We ought not to deceive ourselves. The maritime resources of Great Britain are more substantial and real than those of France and Spain united. Her commerce is more extensive than that of both her rivals; and it is an axiom that the nation which has the most extensive commerce will always have the most powerful marine. Were this argument less convincing the fact speaks for itself; her progress in the course of the last year is an incontestible proof.

It is true France in a manner created a Fleet in a very short space and this may mislead us in the judgment we form of her naval abilities. But if they bore any comparison with those of great Britain how comes it to pass, that with all the force of Spain added she has lost so much ground in so short a time, as now to have scarcely a superiority. We should consider what was done by France as a violent and unnatural effort of the government, which for want of sufficient foundation, cannot continue to operate proportionable effects.

In modern wars the longest purse must chiefly determine the event. I fear that of the enemy will be found to be so. Though the government is deeply in debt and of course poor, the nation is rich and their riches afford a fund which will not be easily exhausted. Besides, their system of public credit is such that it is capable of greater exertions than that of any other nation. Speculatists have been a long time foretelling its downfall, but we see no symptoms of the catastrophe being very near. I am persuaded it will at least last out the war, and then, in the opinion of many of the best politicians it will be a national advantage. If the war should terminate successfully the crown will have acquired such influence and power that it may attempt any thing, and a bankruptcy will probably be made the ladder to climb to absolute authority. Administration may perhaps wish to drive matters to this issue; at any rate they will not be restrained by an apprehension of it from forcing the resources of the state. It will promote their present purposes on which their all is at stake and it may pave the way to triumph more effectually over the constitution. With this disposition I have no doubt that ample means will be found to prosecute the war with the greatest vigor.

France is in a very different position. The abilities of her present Financier[2] have done wonders. By a wise administration of the revenues aided by advantageous loans he has avoided the necessity of additional taxes. But I am well informed, if the war continues another campaign he will be obliged to have recourse to the taxes usual in time of war which are very heavy, and which the people of France are not in a condition to endure for any duration. When this necessity commences France makes war on ruinous terms; and England from her individual wealth' will find much greater facility in supplying her exigencies.

Spain derives great wealth from her mines, but not so great as is generally imagined. Of late years the profits to government is essentially diminished. Commerce and industry are the best mines of a nation; both which are wanting to her. I am told her treasury is far from being so well filled as we have flattered ourselves. She is also much divided on the propriety of the war. There is a strong party against it. The temper of the nation is too sluggish to admit of great exertions, and tho' the Courts of the two kingdoms are closely linked together, there never has been in any of their wars a perfect harmony of measures, nor has it been the case in this; which has already been no small detriment to the common cause.

I mention these things to show that the circumstances of our allies as well as our own call for peace; to obtain which we must make one great effort this campaign. The present instance of the friendship of the Court of France is attended with every circumstance that can render it important and agreeable; that can interest our gratitude or fire our emulation. If we do our duty we may even hope to make the campaign decisive on this Continent. But we must do our duty in earnest, or disgrace and ruin will attend us. I am sincere in declaring a full persuasion, that the succour will be fatal to us if our measures are not adequate to the emergency.

1. *Writings,* XVIII, 436-38.
2. Jacques Necker, French minister of finance.

XI

Washington may have underestimated French strength. It was sufficient in any case to see him through the victory at Yorktown (where French sailors and troops outnumbered American), though the larger contest can be said to have ended only with the English victory over Napoleon at Waterloo in 1815. With English recognition of American independence in 1783, Washington hoped to leave the world of power, but he could not ignore the possibility that Americans would lose the independence, so precariously won, by allowing their union to disintegrate. The decline of central power that he had warned against in his letter to Benjamin Harrison in 1778 (and in many other letters throughout the war) accelerated as the fighting came to an end. Those who hoped to revive national feeling and national power looked to him for leadership, but he was wary of any move that might be construed as a bid for personal power or that might threaten the supremacy of civil government over the military. The need was not for a war hero to seize the reins that Congress was dropping but to make Congress stronger. In a farewell message to each of the governors of the several states on June 8, 1783, he urged them to submerge local jealousies in giving greater strength to their union, greater power to their Congress.[1]

> . . . it appears to me there is an option still left to the United States of America, that it is in their choice, and depends upon their conduct, whether they will be respectable and prosperous, or contemptable and miserable as a Nation; This is the time of their political probation, this is the moment when the eyes of the whole World are turned upon them, this is the moment to establish or ruin their national Character forever, this is the favorable moment to give such a tone to our Federal Government, as will enable it to answer the ends of its institution, or this may be the ill-fated moment for relaxing the powers of the

67

Union, annihilating the cement of the Confederation, and exposing us to become the sport of European politics, which may play one State against another to prevent their growing importance, and to serve their own interested purposes. For, according to the system of Policy the States shall adopt at this moment, they will stand or fall, and by their confirmation or lapse, it is yet to be decided, whether the Revolution must ultimately be considered as a blessing or a curse: a blessing or a curse, not to the present age alone, for with our fate will the destiny of unborn Millions be involved.

With this conviction of the importance of the present Crisis, silence in me would be a crime; I will therefore speak to your Excellency, the language of freedom and of sincerity, without disguise; I am aware, however, that those who differ from me in political sentiment, may perhaps remark, I am stepping out of the proper line of my duty, and they may possibly ascribe to arrogance or ostentation, what I know is alone the result of the purest intention, but the rectitude of my own heart, which disdains such unworthy motives, the part I have hitherto acted in life, the determination I have formed, of not taking any share in public business hereafter, the ardent desire I feel, and shall continue to manifest, of quietly enjoying in private life, after all the toils of War, the benefits of a wise and liberal Government, will, I flatter myself, sooner or later convince my Countrymen, that I could have no sinister views in delivering with so little reserve, the opinions contained in this Address.

There are four things, which I humbly conceive, are essential to the well being, I may even venture to say, to the existence of the United States as an Independent Power:

1st. An indissoluble Union of the States under one Federal Head.

2dly. A Sacred regard to Public Justice.

3dly. The adoption of a proper Peace Establishment, and

4thly. The prevalence of that pacific and friendly Disposition, among the People of the United States, which will induce them to forget their local prejudices and policies, to make those mutual concessions which are requisite to the general prosperity, and in some instances, to sacrifice their individual advantages to the interest of the Community.

These are the Pillars on which the glorious Fabrick of our Independency and National Character must be supported; Liberty is the Basis, and whoever would dare to sap the foundation, or overturn the Structure, under whatever specious pretexts he may attempt it, will merit the bitterest execration, and the severest punishment which can be inflicted by his injured Country....

Under the first head, altho' it may not be necessary or proper for me in this place to enter into a particular disquisition of the principles of the Union, and to take up the great question which has been frequently agitated, whether it be expedient and requisite for the States to delegate a larger proportion of Power to Congress, or not, Yet it will be a part of my duty, and that of every true Patriot, to assert without reserve, and to insist upon the following positions, That unless the States will suffer Congress to exercise those prerogatives, they [i.e. Congress] are undoubtedly invested with by the Constitution, every thing must very rapidly tend to Anarchy and confusion, That it is indispensable to the happiness of the individual States, that there should be lodged somewhere, a

Supreme Power to regulate and govern the general concerns of the Confederated Republic, without which the Union cannot be of long duration. That there must be a faithfull and pointed compliance on the part of every State, with the late proposals and demands of Congress, or the most fatal consequences will ensue, That whatever measures have a tendency to dissolve the Union, or contribute to violate or lessen the Sovereign Authority, ought to be considered as hostile to the Liberty and Independency of America, and the Authors of them treated accordingly, and lastly, that unless we can be enabled by the concurrence of the States, to participate of the fruits of the Revolution, and enjoy the essential benefits of Civil Society, under a form of Government so free and uncorrupted, so happily guarded against the danger of oppression, as has been devised and adopted by the Articles of Confederation, it will be a subject of regret, that so much blood and treasure have been lavished for no purpose, that so many sufferings have been encountered without a compensation, and that so many sacrifices have been made in vain. Many other considerations might here be adduced to prove, that without an entire conformity to the Spirit of the Union, we cannot exist as an Independent Power; it will be sufficient for my purpose to mention but one or two which seem to me of the greatest importance. It is only in our united Character as an Empire, that our Independence is acknowledged, that our power can be regarded, or our Credit supported among Foreign Nations. The Treaties of the European Powers with the United States of America, will have no validity on a dissolution of the Union. We shall be left nearly in a state of Nature, or we may find by our own unhappy experience, that there is a natural and necessary progression, from the extreme of anarchy to the extreme of Tyranny; and that arbitrary power is most easily established on the ruins of Liberty abused to licentiousness....

If in treating of political points, a greater latitude than usual has been taken in the course of this Address, the importance of the Crisis, and the magnitude of the objects in discussion, must be my apology: It is, however, neither my wish or expectation, that the preceding observations should claim any regard, except so far as they shall appear to be dictated by a good intention, consonant to the immutable rules of Justice; calculated to produce a liberal system of policy, and founded on whatever experience may have been acquired by a long and close attention to public business. Here I might speak with the more confidence from my actual observations, and, if it would not swell this Letter (already too prolix) beyond the bounds I had prescribed myself: I could demonstrate to every mind open to conviction, that in less time and with much less expence than has been incurred, the War might have been brought to the same happy conclusion, if the resourses of the Continent could have been properly drawn forth, that the distresses and disappointments which have very often occurred, have in too many instances, resulted more from a want of energy, in the Continental Government, than a deficiency of means in the particular States. That the inefficiency of measures, arising from the want of an adequate authority in the Supreme Power, from a partial compliance with the Requisitions of Congress in some of the States, and from a failure of punctuality in others, while it tended to damp the zeal of those which were more willing to exert themselves; served also to accumulate the expences of the War, and to frustrate the best concerted Plans, and that the discouragement occasioned by the complicated difficulties and embarrassments, in which our affairs were, by this means involved, would have long ago produced the dissolution of any Army, less patient, less virtuous and less persevering, than that which I have had the honor to command. But while I mention these things, which are notorious facts, as the defects of our Federal Constitution, particularly in the prosecution of a War, I beg it may be understood, that as I have ever taken a pleasure in gratefully acknowledging the assistance and support I have derived from every Class of Citizens, so shall I always be happy to do justice to the unparalleled exertion of the individual States, on many interesting occasions.

I have thus freely disclosed what I wished to make known, before I surrendered up my Public trust to those who committed it to me, the task is now accomplished, I now bid adieu to your Excellency as the Chief Magistrate of your State, at the same time I bid a last farewell to the cares of Office, and all the imployments of public life.

---

1. *Writings*, XXVI, 485-89, 494-95.

XII

Washington, as he promised, retired from public life, but he could not help but be troubled by the continuing failure of the states to adopt more "liberal" views of their own best interests. In private letters he urged everyone he knew to help in moving the country toward a national government worthy of the name. In July, 1783, in a letter to Reverend William Gordon, who was writing the history of the Revolution, Washington explained why he thought a popular constitutional convention was needed to confer real power on the central government.[1]

It now rests with the Confederated Powers [i.e. the United States], by the line of conduct they mean to adopt, to make this Country great, happy, and respectable; or to sink it into littleness; worse perhaps, into Anarchy and Confusion; for certain I am, that unless adequate Powers are given to Congress for the *general* purposes of the Federal Union that we shall soon moulder into dust and become contemptable in the Eyes of Europe, if we are not made the sport of their Politicks; to suppose that the general concern of this Country can be directed by thirteen heads, or one head without competent powers, is a solecism, the bad effects of which every Man who has had the practical knowledge to judge from, that I have, is fully convinced of; tho' none perhaps has felt them in so forcible, and distressing a degree. The People at large, and at a distance from the theatre of Action, who only know that the Machine was kept in motion, and that they are at last arrived at the first object of their Wishes are satisfied with the event, without investigating the causes of the slow progress to it, or of the Expences which have accrued and which they now seem unwilling to pay; great part of which has arisen from that want of energy in the Federal Constitution which I am complaining of, and which I wish to see given to it by a Convention of the People, instead of hearing it remarked that as we have worked through an arduous Contest with the Powers Congress already have (but which, by the by, have been gradually diminishing) why should they be invested with more?

To say nothing of the invisible workings of Providence, which has conducted us through difficulties where no human foresight could point the way; it will appear evident to a close Examiner, that there has been a concatenation of causes to produce this Event; which in all probability at no time, or under any Circumstances, will combine again. We deceive ourselves therefore by this mode of reasoning, and what would be much worse, we may bring ruin upon ourselves by attempting to carry it into practice.

We are known by no other character among Nations than as the United States; Massachusetts or Virginia is no better defined, nor any more thought of by Foreign Powers than the County of Worcester in Massachusetts is by Virginia, or Glouster County in Virginia is by Massachusetts (respectable as they are); and yet these Counties, with as much propriety might oppose themselves to the Laws of the State in wch. they are, as an Individual State can oppose itself to the Federal Government, by which it is, or ought to be bound. Each of these Counties has, no doubt, its local polity and Interests. these should be attended to, and brought before their respective legislatures with all the force their importance merits; but when they come in contact with the general Interest of the State; when superior considerations preponderate in favor of the whole, their Voices should be heard no more;

so should it be with individual States when compared to the Union. Otherwise I think it may properly be asked for what purpose do we farcically pretend to be United? Why do Congress spend Months together in deliberating upon, debating, and digesting plans, which are made as palatable, and as wholesome to the Constitution of this Country as the nature of things will admit of, when some States will pay no attention to them, and others regard them but partially; by which means all those evils which proceed from delay, are felt by the whole; while the compliant States are not only suffering by these neglects, but in many instances are injured most capitally by their own exertions; which are wasted for want of the United effort. A hundd. thousand men coming one after another cannot move a Ton weight; but the united strength of 50 would transport it with ease. so has it been with great part of the expence which has been incurred this War. In a Word, I think the blood and treasure which has been spent in it has been lavished to little purpose, unless we can be better Cemented; and that is not to be effected while so little attention is paid to the recommendations of the Sovereign Power.

To me it would seem not more absurd, to hear a traveller, who was setting out on a long journey, declare he would take no Money in his pocket to defray the Expences of it but rather depend upon chance and charity lest he should misapply it, than are the expressions of so much fear of the powers and means of Congress. For Heavens sake who are Congress? are they not the Creatures of the People, amenable to them for their Conduct, and dependant from day to day on their breath? Where then can be the danger of giving them such Powers as are adequate to the great ends of Government, and to all the general purposes of the Confederation (I repeat the word *genl,* because I am no advocate for their having to do with the particular policy of any State, further than it concerns the Union at large). What may be the consequences if they have not these Powers I am at no loss to guess; and deprecate the worst; for sure I am, we shall, in a little time, become as contemptable in the great Scale of Politicks as we now have it in our power to be respectable; and that, when the band of Union gets once broken, every thing ruinous to our future prospects is to be apprehended; the best that can come of it, in my humble opinion is, that we shall sink into obscurity, unless our Civil broils should keep us in remembrance and fill the page of history with the direful consequences of them.

You say that, Congress loose time by pressing a mode that does not accord with the genius of the People, and will thereby, endanger the Union; and that it is the quantum they want.[2] Permit me to ask if the quantum has not already been demanded? Whether it has been obtained? and whence proceed the accumulated evils, and poignant distresses of many of the public Creditors, particularly in the Army? For my own part I hesitate not a moment to confess, that I see nothing wherein the Union is endangered by the late requisition of that body; but a prospect of much good, justice, and propriety from the compliance with it. I know of no Tax more convenient; none so agreeable, as that which every man may pay, or let it alone as his convenience, abilities, or Inclination shall prompt. I am therefore a warm friend to the Impost.

I can only repeat to you, that whenever Congress shall think proper to open the door of their Archives to you, (which can be best known, and with more propriety discovered through the Delegates of your own State), All my Records and Papers shall be unfolded to your View, and I shall be happy in your Company at Mt. Vernon, while you are taking such Extracts from them, as you may find convenient. It is a piece of respect wch. I think is due to the Sovereign Power to let it take the lead in this business (without any interference of mine). and another reason why I choose to withhold mine, to this epoch is, that I am positive no History of the Revolution can be perfect if the Historiographer has not free access to that fund of Information.

1. *Writings*, XXVII, 49-52.
2. Congress had proposed that the states vest it with the power to collect a five per cent duty on imports into the United States (referred to below as "the Impost"). Since such a power was not included in the Articles of Confederation, unanimous consent of the member states would have been required to confer it on Congress. The measure never achieved such consent. In 1782 Rhode Island had blocked the way; and when the proposal was revived in the following year, New York delayed until 1786 and then attached conditions to its ratification that Congress regarded as tantamount to rejection.

XIII

It took another four years for Americans to persuade themselves that they needed a central government powerful enough to give direction to public policy at home and abroad. During those years Washington's letters to European correspondents expressed his confidence in the country's long-run health, but his letters to close friends grew increasingly alarmed. On August 1, 1786, he wrote both to La Luzerne, the former French envoy to the United States, and to John Jay, the Secretary for Foreign Affairs under the disintegrating United States Congress. The difference between the two letters is instructive.[1]

To La Luzerne

Nothing could be more satisfactory to me than the friendly sentiments...and the generous manner in which you always interest yourself in the happiness and dignity of the United States. I wish I had it in my power to inform you that the several States had fully complied with all the wise requisitions which Congress has made to them on national subjects. But unfortunately for us, this is not yet the case. Altho' for my own part I do not cease to expect that this just policy will ultimately take effect. It is not the part of a good Citizen to despair of the republic: nor ought we to have calculated, that our young Governments would have acquired, in so short a period, all the consistency and solidity, which it has been the work of ages to give to other nations. All the States however, have at length granted the impost; tho' unhappily some of them have granted it under such qualifications, as have hitherto prevented its operation. The greater part of the Union seems to be convinced of the necessity of foederal measures, and of investing Congress with the power of regulating the commerce of the whole. The reasons you offer on this subject are certainly forcible, and I cannot but hope will 'ere long have their due efficacy.

In other respects our internal Governments are daily acquiring strength. The laws have their fullest energy; justice is well administered; robbery, violence or murder is not heard of from Nw. Hampshire to Georgia. The people at large (as far as I can learn) are more industrious than they were before the war. Oeconomy begins, partly from necessity and partly from choice and habit, to prevail. The seeds of population are scattered over an immense tract of western country. In the old States, wch. were the theatres of hostility, it is wonderful to see how soon the ravages of war are repaired. Houses are rebuilt, fields enclosed, stocks of cattle which were destroyed are replaced, and many a desolated territory assumes again the cheerful appearance of cultivation. In many places the vestiges of conflagration and ruin are hardly to be traced. The arts of peace, such as clearing rivers, building bridges, and establishing conveniences for travelling &c. are assiduously promoted. In short, the foundation of a great Empire is laid, and I please myself with a persuasion, that Providence will not leave its work imperfect.

I am sensible that the picture of our situation, which has been exhibited in Europe since the Peace, has been of a very different complexion; but it must be remembered that all the unfavorable features have been much heightened by the medium of the English newspapers thro' which they have been represented. The British still continue to hold the Posts on our frontiers, and affect to charge us with some infractions of the Treaty. On the other hand we retort the accusation. What will be the consequences, is more than I can pretend to predict. To me, however, it appears, that they are playing the same foolish game in commerce that they have lately done in War; that their ill-judged impositions will eventually drive our ships from their ports, wean our attachments to their manufactures, and give to France decided advantages for a commercial connexion with us. To strengthen the alliance and promote the interests of France and America will ever be the favorite object of him, who has the honor to subscribe himself, with every sentiment of attachment, &c.

To John Jay

I am sorry to be assured, of what indeed I had little doubt before, that we have been guilty of violating the treaty in some instances.[2] What a misfortune it is the British should have so well grounded a pretext for their palpable infractions: and what a disgraceful part, out of the choice of difficulties before us, are we to act.

Your sentiments, that our affairs are drawing rapidly to a crisis, accord with my own. What the event will be, is also beyond the reach of my foresight. We have errors to correct; we have probably had too good an opinion of human nature in forming our confederation. Experience has taught us, that men will not adopt and carry into execution measures the best calculated for their own good, without the intervention of a coercive power. I do not conceive we can exist long as a nation without having lodged some where a power, which will pervade the whole Union in as energetic a manner, as the authority of the State Governments extends over the several States.

To be fearful of investing Congress, constituted as that body is, with ample authorities for national purposes, appears to me the very climax of popular absurdity and madness. Could Congress exert them for the detriment of the public, without injuring themselves in an equal or greater proportion? Are not their interests inseparably connected with those of their constituents? By the rotation of appointment, must they not mingle frequently with the mass of Citizens? Is it not rather to be apprehended, if they were possessed of the powers before described, that the individual members would be induced to use them, on many occasions, very timidly and inefficaciously for fear of losing their popularity and future election? We must take human nature as we find it: perfection falls not to the share of mortals. Many are of opinion that Congress have too frequently made use of the suppliant humble tone of requisition, in applications to the States, when they had a right to assert their imperial dignity and command obedience. Be that as it may, requisitions are a perfect nihility where thirteen sovereign independent disunited States are in the habit of discussing and refusing compliance with them at their option. Requisitions are actually little better than a jest and a bye word throughout the land. If you tell the Legislatures they have violated the Treaty of Peace, and invaded the prerogatives of the confederacy, they will laugh in your face. What then is to be done? Things cannot go on in the same train forever. It is much to be feared, as you observe, that the better kind of people, being disgusted with the circumstances, will have their minds prepared for any revolution whatever. We are apt to run from one extreme into another. To anticipate and prevent disastrous contingencies, would be the part of wisdom and patriotism.

What astonishing changes a few years are capable of producing. I am told that even respectable characters speak of a monarchical form of Government without horror. From thinking proceeds speaking, thence to acting is often but a single step. But how irrevocable and tremendous! what a triumph of our enemies to verify their predictions! what a triumph for the advocates of despotism to find that we are incapable of governing ourselves, and that systems founded on the basis of equal liberty are merely ideal and fallacious! Would to God that wise measures may be taken in time to avert the consequences we have but too much reason to apprehend.

Retired as I am from the world I, frankly acknowledge I cannot feel myself an unconcerned spectator.
Yet, having happily assisted in bringing the Ship into
Port, and having been fairly discharged; it is not my
business to embark again on a sea of troubles. Nor
could it be expected, that my sentiments and opinions
would have much weight on the minds of my Countrymen; they have been neglected, tho' given as a last
legacy in the most solumn manner.[3] I had then
perhaps some claims to public attention. I consider
myself as having none at present.

1. *Writings,* XXVIII, 499-503.
2. The treaty of peace that ended the War for Independence
   had provided that "Creditors on either Side shall meet with
   no lawful impediment to the Recovery of the full Value in
   Sterling Money of all bona fide Debts heretofore con-
   tracted." Many states had passed laws that violated this
   provision, and Congress was helpless to prevent the viola-
   tions. The British violated other provisions of the treaty by
   carrying away slaves who had fled to their lines and by
   refusing to give up the fortified posts that they held in the
   Northwest territory.
3. See above, his farewell message to the governors of the
   states, June 8, 1783.

XIV

Washington's estimate of his own influence was too
modest. His presiding role at the Philadelphia Convention
the next year and his approval of the new Constitution
went far toward securing its adoption. When he became
the first president under it, his own prestige both at home
and abroad bolstered that of the new government.
Washington's letters from this period are less numerous
and less revealing than those of his earlier years. In conducting the government he seems to have relied heavily on
oral communications, leaving paper work to his cabinet

officers. His greatest legacy to the nation was the policy of neutrality expressed in his farewell address. The address was mainly in the words of Alexander Hamilton, but the policy was Washington's, formulated before he became president and expressed in the following passages from a succession of letters from 1788 to 1797.[1]

To Thomas Jefferson, January 1, 1788

...from appearances (as given to us) it is not improbable but that a pretty general war will be kindled in Europe. should this be the case, we shall feel more than ever the want of an efficient general Government to regulate our Commercial concerns, to give us a national respectability, and to connect the political views and interests of the several States under one head in such a manner as will effectually prevent them from forming seperate, improper, or indeed any connection, with the European powers which can involve them in their political disputes. For our situation is such as makes it not only unnecessary, but extremely imprudent for us to take a part in their quarrels; and whenever a contest happens among them, if we wisely and properly improve the advantages which nature has given us, we may be benifitted by their folly, provided we conduct ourselves with circumspection and under proper restrictions, for I perfectly agree with you, that an extensive speculation, a spirit of gambling, or the introduction of any thing which will divert our attention from Agriculture, must be extremely prejudicial, if not ruinous to us. but I conceive under an energetic general Government such regulations might be made, and such measures taken, as would render this Country the asylum of pacific and industrious characters from all parts of Europe, would encourage the cultivation of

83

the Earth by the high price which its products would command, and would draw the wealth, and wealthy men of other Nations, into our bosom, by giving security to property, and liberty to its holders. I have the honor &c.

To the Marquis de LaFayette, August 11, 1790

It seems to be our policy to keep in the situation in which nature has placed us, to observe a strict neutrality, and to furnish others with those good things of subsistence, which they may want, and which our fertile land abundantly produces, if circumstances and events will permit us so to do....Gradually recovering from the distresses in which the war left us, patiently advancing in our task of civil government, unentangled in the crooked politics of Europe, wanting scarcely any thing but the free navigation of the Mississippi (which we must have and as certainly shall have as we remain a Nation) I have supposed, that, with the undeviating exercise of a just, steady, and prudent national policy, we shall be the gainers, whether the powers of the old world may be in peace or war, but more especially in the latter case. In that case our importance will certainly encrease, and our friendship be courted.

To Gouverneur Morris, July 28,1791

The change of systems, which have so long prevailed in Europe, will, undoubtedly, affect us in a degree proportioned to our political or commercial connexions with the several nations of it. But I trust we shall never so far lose sight of our own interest and happiness as to become, unnecessarily, a party in their political disputes. Our local situation enables us to keep that state with them, which otherwise could not, perhaps, be preserved by human wisdom. The present moment seems pregnant with great events; But, as you observe, it is beyond the ken of mortal foresight to determine what will be the result of those changes which are either making or contemplated in the general system of Europe. Altho' as fellow-men we sincerely lament the disorders, oppressions, and incertitude which frequently attend national events, and which our European brethren must feel; yet we cannot but hope that it will terminate very much in favor of the Rights of man; and that a change there will be favorable to this Country I have no doubt. For, under the former system we were seen either in the distresses of war, or viewed after the peace in a most unfavorable light through the medium of our distracted state. In neither point could we appear of much consequence among Nations. And should affairs continue in Europe in the same state they were when these impressions respecting us were received, it would not be an easy matter to remove the prejudices imbibed against us. A change of system will open a new view of things, and we shall then burst upon them, as it were with redoubled advantages.

Should we under the present state of affairs form connexions, other than we now have, with any European powers, much must be considered in effecting them, on the score of our increasing importance as a Nation; and, at the same time, should a treaty be formed with a Nation whose circumstances may not at this moment be very bright much delicacy would be necessary in order to shew that no undue advantages were taken on that account. For unless treaties are mutually beneficial to the Parties, it is in vain to hope for a continuance of them beyond the moment when the one which conceives itself to be over-reached is in a situation to break off the connexion. And I believe it is among nations as with individuals, the party taking advantage of the distresses of another will lose infinitely more in the opinion of mankind and in subsequent events than he will gain by the stroke of the moment.

To Patrick Henry, October 9, 1795

I can most religiously aver I have no wish, that is incompatible with the dignity, happiness and true interest of the people of this country. My ardent desire is, and my aim has been (as far as depended upon the Executive Department,) to comply strictly with *all* our engagemts. foreign and domestic, but to keep the U States free from *political* connexions with *every* other Country. To see that they *may be* independent of *all,* and under the influence of *none.* In a word, I want an *American* character, that the powers of Europe may be convinced we act for *ourselves* and not for *others;* this in my judgement, is the only way to be respected abroad and happy at home and not by becoming the partizans of Great Britain or France, create dissensions, disturb the public tranquillity, and destroy, perhaps for ever the cement wch. binds the Union.

To William Heath, May 20, 1797

I hope, as you do, that, notwithstanding our Political horison is much overcast, the wisdom, temper and firmness of the Government (supported by the great mass of the People) will dispel the threatning clouds, and that all will end without any shedding of Blood. To me, this is so demonstrable that not a particle of doubt would dwell on my mind relative thereto if our Citizens would advocate their own cause instead of that of any other Nation under the Sun; that is instead of being Frenchmen, or Englishmen, in Politics, they would be Americans; indignant at every attempt of either, or any other power to establish an influence in our Councils, or that should presume to sow the seeds of distrust or disunion among ourselves. No policy, in my opinion, can be more clearly demonstrated, than that we should do justice to *all* but have no political connexions with *any* of the European Powers, beyond those which result from and serve to regulate our Commerce with them. Our own experience (if it has not already had this effect) will soon convince us that *disinterested* favours, or friendship from any Nation whatever, is too novel to be calculated on; and there will always be found a wide difference between the words and actions of any of them.

---

1. *Writings,* XXIX, 350-51; XXXI, 87-88, 327-28; XXXIV, 335; XXXV, 449.

NOTES

1. Silas Deane to Elizabeth Deane, July 1, 1775, in Paul H. Smith, ed., *Letters of Delegates to Congress 1774-1789* (Washington, D.C., 1976-   ), I, 567.

2. David Ramsay, *The History of the American Revolution* (Philadelphia, 1789), II, 316.

3. Max Farrand, ed., *The Records of the Federal Convention of 1787* (New Haven, 1911), III, 85-86.

4. To William Woodford, November 10, 1775, John C. Fitzpatrick, ed., *The Writings of George Washington from the Original Manuscript Sources, 1745-1799* (Washington, D.C., 1931-44), IV, 80-81. Subsequent references, unless otherwise indicated, are to volumes of this work.

5. To William Pearce, December 18, 1793, XXXIII, 191.

6. To Thomas Nelson, September 2, 1777, IX, 164.

7. To de Grasse, September 25, 1781, XXIII, 136-39; cf. to Noah Webster, July 31, 1788, XXX, 26-28.

8. To the President of Congress, September 13, 1777, IX, 215.

9. To Henry Laurens, October 3, 1778, XIII, 15.

10. To the President of Congress, December 22, 1777, X, 186. Cf. to same, August 10, September 13, 1777, IX, 46, 215; to Lafayette, May 18, 1778, XI, 419.

11. To the President of Congress, August 20, 1780, XIX, 408-409.

12. To same, February 18, 1776, IV, 336; to Patrick Henry, November 13, 1777, X, 52.

13. His views on this subject are most explicit in various letters to Bryan Fairfax and George William Fairfax in the summer of 1774, III, 221-42; to Bryan Fairfax, March 1, 1778, X, 2-5; and to George William Fairfax, July 10, 1783, XXVII, 57-60.

14. To Joseph Reed, January 31, 1776, IV, 297.

15. To Lewis Nicola, May 22, 1782, XXIV, 272. Cf. to John Jay, August 1, 1786, XXVIII, 503.

16. To Sir Edward Newenham, November 25, 1785, XXVIII, 323.

17. To the President of Congress, November 11, 1778, XIII, 223-44.

18. To Henry Laurens, November 14, 1778, XIII, 254-57.

19. To Fielding Lewis, July 6, 1780, XIX, 131. Cf. to Thomas Jefferson, August 14, 1780, to the President of Congress, August 20, 1780, XIX, 373-75, 408-411; to John Mathews, October 4, 1780, to John Cadwalader, October 5, 1780, Circular to the States, October 18, 1780, to George Mason, October 22, 1780, to William Fitzhugh, October 22, 1780, to Benjamin Lincoln, December 11, 1780, XX, 113-16, 122-23, 206-211, 242, 246-47, 461; to John Parke Custis, February 28, 1781, to William Fitzhugh, March 25, 1781, XXI, 319, 374-77; to Fielding Lewis, June 28, 1781, to William Fitzhugh, August 8, 1781, XXII, 282-83, 480-81.

20. To the Committee of Cooperation, June 11, 1780, XVIII, 505; to Jonathan Trumbull, June 27, 1780, to Daniel Brodhead, July 4, 1780, XIX, 81-82, 119; to the President of Congress, September 15, 1780, Circular to the States, October 18, 1780, XX, 49-52, 205.

21. To John Laurens, January 15, April 9, 1781, XXI, 109, 438-39.

22. Washington had confided to William Fitzhugh, on March 25, 1781, that the war "is like to become a War of finance, and that no funds within our reach can support it long." XXI, 375.

23. To Joseph Reed, May 28, 1780, XVIII, 436-37.

24. To James McHenry, August 22, 1785, XXVIII, 227-30.

25. To William Grayson, August 22, 1785, XXVIII, 233-34.

26. To Joseph Reed, July 4, 1780, XIX, 114.

27. To Henry Lee, October 31, 1786, XXIX, 34.

28. To James Madison, November 5, 1786, XXIX, 52.

29. To Benjamin Lincoln, March 23, 1787, XXIX, 181-82.

30. To John Augustine Washington, June 15, 1783, XXVII, 13.

31. To James Duane, April 10, 1785, XXVIII, 124.

32. To Patrick Henry, October 9, 1795, XXXIV, 335; to Thomas Jefferson, July 6, to Charles Cotesworth Pinckney, July 8, 1796, XXXV, 120, 129.

33. To Catharine Macaulay Graham, he explained that his

wife's "wishes coincide with my own as to simplicity of dress, and everything which can tend to support propriety of character without partaking of the follies of luxury and ostentation." January 9, 1790, XXX, 498. Cf. to David Stuart, July 26, 1789, XXX, 359-63.

34. In his suppression of the Whiskey Rebellion in western Pennsylvania, Washington was particularly concerned to show to Europeans how firmly the United States government could act. After it was over he wrote to Edmund Pendleton (January 22, 1795, XXXIV, 98-99): "I hope, and believe, that the spirit of anarchy in the western counties of this State (to quell which the force of the Union was called for) is *entirely* subdued; and altho' to effect it, the community has been saddled with a considerable expence, yet I trust no money could have been more advantageously expended; both as it respects the internal peace and welfare of *this* country, and the impression it will make on *others.* The spirit with which the Militia turned out, in support of the Constitution, and the laws of our country, at the same time that it does them immortal honor, is the most conclusive refutation that could have been given to the assertions of Lord Sheffield, and the prediction of others of his cast, that without the protection of Great Britain, we should be unable to govern ourselves; and would soon be involved in anarchy and confusion. They will see that republicanism is not the phantom of a deluded imagination: on the contrary, that under no form of government, will laws be better supported, liberty and property better secured, or happiness be more effectually dispensed to mankind."

35. To the Members of the Volunteer Association and other inhabitants of the Kingdom of Ireland who have lately arrived in the City of New York, December 2, 1783, XXVII, 253-54; to Lucretia Wilhelmina Van Winter, March 30, to David Humphreys, July 25, to Lafayette, July 25, 1785, XXVIII, 119-20, 202-203, 206; to Thomas Jefferson, January 1, to John Armstrong, April 25, 1788, XXIX, 350-51, 467.

36. James Madison expressed Washington's views well when Washington had him draft a farewell address (never used) at the end of Washington's first term. Madison would have

had Washington observe "that Nations as well as individuals, act for their own benefit, and not for the benefit of others, unless both interests happen to be assimilated (and when that is the case there requires no contract to bind them together)." (XXXV, 57) In other words, treaties were feasible only when the interests of both parties coincided and when that was the case a treaty was scarcely needed except to give form to relationships. Washington sent this passage to Hamilton along with some others from Madison's draft for use in the address that Hamilton drafted at the end of Washington's second term, the draft that was actually used. But Hamilton did not work this observation into the final version.

37. To Gouverneur Morris, July 28, 1791, XXXI, 328. Cf. to same, March 25, 1793, XXXII, 402-403.

38. To Alexander Hamilton, July 13, to Edmund Randolph, July 22, 1795, XXXIV, 237-40, 244. Washington was convinced from the beginning that the British would retain the Northwest posts. To the President of Congress, August 22, 1785, to Lafayette, May 10, 1786, XXVIII, 231, 422-23.

39. During the 1780s Washington had been wary of insisting on the right to navigate the Mississippi, because he feared that if such a right were obtained it might attach the western settlers by commercial ties to the Spanish in New Orleans. In those years he devoted himself to fostering the construction of canals and waterways between the Ohio River and the James and the Potomac, with a view to binding the West to the East. He was convinced, in any case, that "Whenever the new States become so populous and so extended to the westward, as really to need it, there will be no power which can deprive them of the use of the Mississippi." (To Henry Lee, June 18, 1786, XXVIII, 460). By 1789, however, though the canals were not completed, it was apparent that the western settlers might be pushed toward Spain, if the United States did *not* insist on navigation of the Mississippi. Washington accordingly changed his view of what diplomatic position should be followed, and expressed the opinion to his cabinet officers "that the claim of the United States to this Navigation ought not to be weakened by any negotiation whatsoever." (XXX, 487).

INDEX